10 MIND HACKS
— FOR —
QUICKER
EMOTIONAL HEALING

BENJY SHERER

10 Mind Hacks for Quicker Emotional Healing.

An in-depth guide and 10+ practical tools and techniques that you can use to manipulate the programming of your subconscious mind, so that you can accelerate your inner healing, master your emotions and steer your life in a better direction.

This book has been self-published (April 2021).

If any book agents or publishers are interested in this work, please get in touch.

BSherer@BenjyShererCoaching.com

"I think, therefore I am."

RENE DESCARTES.

"I feel, therefore I am."

ME

*Time to get out of our heads and
back into our hearts.*

ABOUT THE AUTHOR

There is a fine line between emotional awareness and spiritual awakening, and that is where Benjy thrives as a mentor and teacher. Guiding people to emotional mastery, Benjy bridges the gaps between psychology, spirituality and philosophy. Those three realms are all intrinsically connected in Benjy's completely unique - and yet intuitively and compellingly simple - approach to self-love and emotional mastery.

Growing up with a deep existential need for answers, Benjy's academic background was in Philosophy and World Religions, but that academic search left him pessimistic at the soul level about our ultimate role in this universe and the purpose of life. It wasn't until after a dark night of the soul and a spiritual awakening of his own that he was forced to dive more deeply into his own inner healing, in order to rediscover his true purpose and learn the skills, tools, and techniques that he teaches to clients today.

His overall approach is about "Feelings First", referring to the notion that you can master your emotions directly, without the need for deep intellectual analysis, ultra-spiritual practices, or pharmaceutical medications. He teaches people how to connect directly with the emotions and sensations of their body - without fear, guilt or shame - and to allow these feelings to run through them so that they can be truly released. It's about building emotional muscle, not seeking rational answers.

As he says, emotional healing is NOT an intellectual activity.

CONTENTS

INTRODUCTION   1

1: *Programming Subroutines into your Brain*   7

2: *Give Your Brain a Cookie*   19

3: *Take Responsibility*   27

4: *Affirmation Hacks*   35

5: *Stop Saying That!*   45

6: *Put Your Feelings First*   76

7: *Your Physical Reality*   91

8: *Accept the 'Supernatural'*   103

9: *Frequency Manipulation*   119

10: *Manifesting Scripts*   131

11: *How this all fits into the Healing Journey*   159

12: *Next Steps*   169

13: *Transformations I've Seen*   171

Conclusion   175

INTRODUCTION

Hello, everyone!

Thank you so much for joining me. It is an honor and a pleasure to be able to share my wisdom with the world and to know that it resonates with so many of you. I'm truly grateful.

I'll be honest with you... I never exactly chose this line of work. I just naturally gravitated to it. The universe just pushed me into it, and as it did it became more and more clear that I had actually been preparing for this my whole life. The wisdom that I share in this book, in my videos, in my courses, etc... These were all things that I brought with me into this world, and that I was destined to share. This is why I'm here. I ran from it and tried to play the regular 3D game for a while, but fate caught up with me and here I am, fulfilling my soul's mission by helping as many people as possible heal their wounds and raise their consciousness.

So, thank you for giving me your precious time and attention and allowing me to fulfill my purpose by guiding you towards your own evolution. I look forward to helping you master your mind a little bit better with the 10 Mind Hacks that we are going to be going over in this book, and helping you get one step closer to true emotional mastery and freedom in your life.

If you are reading these words right now, it should be because you are on an inner journey of sorts and you are looking to accelerate your progress on that journey. Maybe you look at it as an awakening, maybe just as a spiritual journey in general, or maybe

1

you see it as an emotional healing journey to overcome the wounds and cycles of your past. Whichever wording you choose to use, each of those are actually the same thing. They are all just different lenses of interpreting the same concept. You are trying to overcome your 'human programming' and you're ready to evolve into something more, something not restricted by fear, guilt, shame, and anger the way that you used to be. You are ready to step into the version of you that you know you were meant to be, or - perhaps more aptly - you are ready to finally reveal and release that full version of yourself onto the world.

The idea behind this book is that - hopefully - by now you are starting to realize that you have been passively allowing your brain to be programmed your whole life in ways that you never noticed before. Hopefully you are starting to recognize false limiting beliefs, unfounded negative thought cycles and patterns, tendencies towards self-harming, sabotaging behavior in your own life, over-sensitivity to certain emotional triggers that have you acting against your own self-interest, and - overall - just all sorts of unhelpful patterns going on inside your own head that are keeping you stuck in your life.

You're also starting to recognize that you have the power to change these things, or - at least - that you should. You're starting to go through this awakening. Whether you realize it or not and whether you're comfortable calling it that or not... that's what it is. There are latent parts of yourself that have been buried inside of you your whole life - stuffed down underneath all of your trauma, pain, and fear - and they are slowly starting to come online again.

If they weren't, then you would be just as blind to your old patterns and behaviors right now as you used to be and you wouldn't be here reading this book and seeking change. You're starting to become aware, though, and the more that you progress on this healing journey the more aware you will become, raising your consciousness even more, day by day.

So, if you're reading this book - I want to let you know that this journey will take you into a whole new life, and most likely, can take you so much further than you are ready to realize just yet. It really goes beyond the limits of what you used to think was possible, so it's hard to wrap your mind around when you're still working through it. You will first need to start changing a lot of false, limiting beliefs before you can even recognize the lengths that you can go to through this inner mastery journey. The scope is far beyond what you can recognize from within your old programming.

How far it takes you though, will be up to you. If you keep going and don't get stuck or lost in the illusion that you've healed everything you need to heal at any point, you can keep progressing until you attain a fairly super-human perspective on your life - and on the world - that will keep you operating at peak performance towards the life of your dreams and enjoying every moment of it 100 times more than you used to.

A lot of people start this journey and get stuck at what I like to call the 'Novice Delusion'. When you begin your awakening or healing journey, it's like... for the first time in your life... you can FINALLY see the subconscious cycles that have been controlling you. Except, what you see when you begin this journey is actually only the very tip of the iceberg. You're seeing the subconscious behaviors and patterns that make sense to the strictly logical 'human' mind you've been operating under so far, but there is SO MUCH more going on that you are going to need to retrain your brain to be able to recognize before you can even begin to change it. You need to change the way that you think about and understand your behavior and the universe around you, before you can even unlock the next level of your healing journey.

So, a lot of people deal with that tip of the iceberg stuff and think that they have completed their inner healing; and they walk around in their lives still getting angry, frustrated, jealous, or upset, but they've stopped trying to progress on this healing journey because they think that they've dealt with everything. Really, they've only dealt with the part of the iceberg that was sticking up out of the water and they're just refusing to recognize that there is anything deeper left to be healed.

They are under the delusion of having healed their wounds, not recognizing that the very fact that they are still getting triggered into those negative emotional frequencies regularly is all the evidence they need to see that they haven't. If anxiety, fear, anger , etc... still have their grasps on you, then you still have plenty more to heal. Simple as that! If you continue far enough on this inner healing journey, you can become emotionally invulnerable. At peace. Buddha-like. Most of us won't reach THAT level, but that is what we're aiming towards and where I'm trying to get you.

Don't underestimate the power of this healing. Don't stop. Every moment of every day your triggers are revealing themselves to you. Any moment of emotional distress that you experience is pointing you in the direction of where you need healing. This is a good thing. Don't run from it. Follow your triggers into your healing and into your heart. That is where the next level of your life is waiting.

In order to help move you as far along this healing journey as possible and in order to do it as quickly and painlessly as possible, we are going to employ what I like to call 'Mind Hacks'. These Mind Hacks operate in just the same way that hacking a computer works. We are going to find exploits and backdoors into the way that our brains program themselves, and take advantage of them to trick our brains into doing what we actually want them to do. We are going to manipulate the ways that our brains form and create associations so that we can train them to adopt this new perspective that we are trying to install into ourselves as quickly as possible.

If you're reading these words right now, then hopefully you've already read my book *Feelings First Shadow Work: A Simple Approach to Self Love and Emotional Mastery*. These mind hacks are meant to be paired with and used alongside the wisdom of that book,

4

where we dove deep into the nature of our harmful emotional cycles and the 'Feelings First' approach to inner healing. While you can certainly use the Mind Hacks in this book without knowing that stuff, they won't be half as effective at truly changing your reality as they could be if you put them together with the higher perspective of what this is all about. Whatever you are trying to master in this life, the 'how' is only going to get you so far unless you pair it with the 'why'.

The methods and techniques taught in this book are meant to complement the higher perspective conceptual wisdom that was taught in that first one. They will provide an opportunity to start practicing the skills needed to take control of your conscious and subconscious mind and to give you some of the strength and foundation you'll be using when diving into the deeper emotional healing journey towards freedom from fear, doubt, guilt, anxiety, etc.

The Mind Hacks presented in this book are meant to be part of a larger journey of self-love and shadow work. Feel free to enjoy them on their own, of course. They will certainly still provide you with a lot of benefit no matter how you use them. Plus, you'll find a lot of helpful wisdom in this book behind the actual hacks that you are going to learn.

This book isn't just a short list of tricks. I mean... Some of them are short, but this book will also offer a deep dive into the explanations behind a lot of them and offer insight into how your mind works and why these mental exploits are effective. This book will help explain a lot about how the reprogramming of your mind actually happens, how you can take advantage of the way your brain works to accelerate your healing, and how these healing techniques impact our brains and our hearts to move us towards change.

If you want to truly maximize and accelerate your healing as much as possible though, make sure that you check out the *'Feelings First Shadow Work'* book as well. You can get it at http://BenjyShererCoaching.com/ffbook. It even comes with a 21-day journaling guide to help get you started.

It is also available on Amazon or on Audible.

If you pair these two books together, you will jumpstart and accelerate your inner healing immensely.

I also just want to give you a little 'heads up' about how this book will go. The first few Mind Hacks that we are going to go over are the most practical and easy to implement. They are short, to-the-point, and very straight forward. They are almost list-style mind hacks that don't require deep dives into intense topics. As we progress through the book, we will start getting deeper into esoteric concepts about the deep programming of our minds and on spiritual and universal ideas. Especially if you are interested in Law of Attraction, Manifesting, and other spiritual concepts like that, you are going to want to stick with me through to the end of the book. So, enjoy the short and easy-to-implement Mind Hacks at the beginning, and prepare for some more mind-blowing revelations by the end.

So... other than this brief intro here, I see no need to beat about the bush or add any extra fluff to this book. I say we dive right on into it with Mind hack #1!

Programming Subroutines into your Brain

I'd like to start with this one because it is simple, short and easy to understand and implement. It is also the one that truly sparked the idea for this book, as it is one of the tricks that most exemplifies the whole notion of 'hacking your brain'.

Please bear with me... it might sound a little complex at the beginning, but I'm going to make it very straight forward.

The idea behind this first one is simple - this healing journey is about over-writing negative programming in our brains and training new neural pathways so that, even when we get triggered and slip into auto-pilot mode because our emotions take over, the most natural path for our brains to follow will be a path of love and compassion, instead of one based on fear and defensiveness, like the ones we've been subconsciously following our whole lives. You've spent a lifetime programming old habits and neural-pathways, and now we are trying to avoid operating on our old programming and to start installing new conscious programming instead.

In order to do this, we need to consciously bring our attention to the patterns that used to fly under the radar so that we can actively push our brains to form new connections and pave new neural-pathways.

This means that, over and over again, we also need to bring our conscious mind's attention back to something new that we are trying to program into ourselves. There are the old habits that used to happen naturally that we are trying to avoid, versus the new habits that we are trying to adapt and integrate. We need to consistently refocus on the new programming that we are trying to implement, to prevent our brains from naturally flowing back into the old patterns, unintentionally reinforcing old habits that we want to change.

In order to help us accelerate this process, we need to find a way to remind ourselves to think of something or to perform a check or an action as we move through our day to day lives. We might - for example - want to constantly remind ourselves to fix our posture, to take a deep breath, to say a mantra, etc. These are things that we are trying to program into ourselves because they help us practice mindfulness, or they help keep us calm and in charge of our emotions, etc. They are practices that are essential to our inner growth and evolution because they bring us back into the moment and help us develop a sense of inner peace, well-being and self-awareness.

No matter how much we know that we want to move in a particular direction, however, we are constantly getting distracted by the world around us and we forget to do these things (despite how quickly and easily they can be done), and so we need a way to bring ourselves back to our intended actions as often as possible.

Think about how this works with generic meditation. Standard mindfulness meditations have us focusing in on our breath to connect us to the present moment. We are meant to focus on the sensations of our breath, how it moves through our nose and mouth, how our stomach rises and falls, how our lungs expand and contract, etc. Keeping our focus on these sensations helps us ground ourselves into the present moment and this is what we are actively trying to practice. Inevitably, though, we continually get distracted, lose focus, and our thoughts start cycling around about other things going on in our lives. Our goal is - as often as possible - to merely notice that we got distracted, to be ok with that, and to bring our attention back to our breath.

When we are not in meditation, however, it is trickier to notice that we are getting distracted from something and to bring our brain's attention back to what we were focusing on, because - in life - we believe that the things that distract us are of actual importance and we get lost in the practical problem-solving mindset that we have been operating under throughout or lives. We believe the outside world to be more real than our inner worlds, and so, when something comes up in the external world that distracts us from the inner journey we are on, we believe that we absolutely need to solve that external problem before turning our attention back to what we were working on internally.

In other words, in meditation it's relatively easy to realize that we got distracted, that we're no longer focusing on our breath and to remember that focusing on the breath was the goal - so we should just bring ourselves back to it. In your day-to-day life, though, when we get distracted from these inner training regimens we had put ourselves onto, it is much harder to notice and realize that we got distracted and to bring ourselves back to them because we are truly and deeply lost in this 3D game that we are playing. We are ultimately invested in it, and that makes us lose focus of what is really important. There's so much more going on when we are walking through our regular lives than there is while we are in meditation, which makes it very hard to stick to the new programming we are trying to install into ourselves.

This ease of distraction and difficulty in remembering to reprogram new habits into yourself is what you are trying to overcome with this first mind hack. You are trying to find ways to bring your conscious mind's attention back to something that you are trying to program into yourself, by attaching this new internal action or behavior to something outside of you, so that these 'distractions' from the outside world can actually work in your favor. You are going to train your brain to react in a helpful way to events that generally hold no meaning for you, so that you can use these events to keep you on track.

You are going to assign new 'subroutines' in your brain regarding your inner work to external circumstances and events so that this external 'distraction' ends up bringing your conscious attention back to your inner work. I know that sounds complicated right now, but just stick with me, it's actually ridiculously simple.

> **You are going to simply take advantage of the way that your brain makes associations, to help remind you of these 'inner work' tasks as often as you can. That's all!**

It is possible - and shockingly easy - to program your brain to use any common day to day event that you experience regularly to trigger a particular response that you want to have. You can train your brain to create the pattern that 'when event A happens, it triggers event B', where 'event B' is something that you want to remind yourself of as often as possible. This is what I call 'programming a subroutine' because you are instructing your brain to perform a secondary action any time it experiences an initial triggering event.

Programming subroutines into your brain is shockingly easy.

All you have to do is pick an event you want to associate this new habit and subroutine to and consciously attach the triggering event to this new subroutine by literally talking to your brain.

Let's say that you want to remind yourself to think about birds as often as possible, and let's say that you have a job where you have to wash your hands a lot. Next time you're washing your hands, just think or say aloud to yourself "every time I'm washing my hands I will think about birds". Say that a couple of times and think about birds while you wash your hands.

Do that consciously the next three to five times that you wash your hands and it will start getting ingrained in you to the point that you won't be able to wash your hands without at least being reminded of the fact that you created this subroutine in your brain. From that point on, it will keep on happening. Every time you wash your hands your brain will simultaneously shoot neurons down this associated pathway. The pathways of 'hand washing' and 'birds' are now connected in your mind because it has simultaneously fired neurons down both of those pathways several times and it has formed an unconscious association between the two.

This association will remain and this subroutine will continue to play itself out for as long as you support it and encourage it to.

For example, if you attempt to program this subroutine but every time it comes up you ignore it or push it away, then it will fade quickly enough. If you're washing your hands and you get reminded about birds but you then think to yourself, "no, now is not a good time. I don't want to think about this right now", then this subroutine will stop working. Your brain will learn that this secondary action isn't important and the association will fade over time.

Alternately though, if every time it comes up you go "Oh, awesome!", congratulate yourself for the fact that this subroutine hack actually worked and proceed to think about birds (because that's what you wanted to happen), you will encourage your brain to continue running this subroutine every time the initial trigger happens. Every time you allow the pattern to play itself out you help your brain to pave that pathway a little more deeply so that it becomes more and more natural for your neurons to flow in that direction the next time around.

To put it simply, every time the initial triggering event happens, your brain will ask you "should I perform this subroutine?" If you continue to say "yes" when it (subconsciously) asks this question, it will learn to perform this subroutine more naturally again and again. You are training your brain what you want it to do. Your brain is pretty obedient like that, actually... you just never realized that you could do this.

All that you need to do is tell it what you want it to do, and then support and encourage it when it follows this new pathway. You also need to avoid any shame cycles when you fail to perform this new subroutine, but I will talk about that in the next chapter. All you need to do for now is pick a triggering event in your day-to-day life (e.g., every time I see a blue car, every time I tie my shoe, every time I have an itch, etc.) and tell your brain that whenever this happens you want to remind yourself of some other thought, emotion, action, habit, etc.

Say this to your brain a few times when that triggering event happens and it will form this association much more quickly and easily than you will believe. It really is that simple and now your brain is following the programming you intentionally installed into it, helping you move in the direction that you want to in your life. It's like your brain has just been waiting for you to give it orders this whole time, but you never did... so it started fooling around and succumbing to negative patterns. Now, you're finally ready to be the leader your brain has always wanted you to be, and it is all too eager and anxious to follow your commands.

1B - Activating the Power of Your Emotions.

To increase the effectiveness of this hack, you should make sure that you practice being actively proud of yourself or pleasantly surprised whenever this subroutine comes up. You should congratulate yourself and rejoice in the good feelings of making progress in your life when you notice this subroutine playing itself out.

Every time you actively congratulate yourself for it and allow yourself to feel good because this worked, you are activating not only the conscious/logical/rational pathways in your brain (the parts of you that consciously notice the triggering event and the new programming) but you are also activating the emotional part of your brain which operates at a more subconscious level. By doing this, you'll be paving this new pathway even more deeply because the positive emotions attached to your thoughts in the moment carry with them a far stronger frequency than the thoughts themselves.

Emotions are always more powerful when it comes to programming our minds than our thoughts are. This is a major element behind the *'Feelings First'* approach to Self Love and Shadow Work discussed in my other book and will be a major theme in this book as well. Connecting directly to our emotions is a way of bypassing the superficial, conscious and logical brain, in order to activate and reprogram the deeper parts of our psyche that have REALLY been in charge this whole time.

The emotions are of a higher order of 'reality' than the thoughts, and they are far more effective at paving pathways in your brain. As much as possible then, you want to connect to positive emotions to help you program new patterns. As long as you continue to follow the subroutine when it comes up and encourage yourself emotionally when it does, this subroutine will keep playing itself out and embedding itself more deeply until performing this new action becomes second nature.

Practicing and reinforcing a positive emotion in relation to this subroutine will help it ingrain itself more deeply, more quickly, and more efficiently. This applies to everything that you are going to be learning in this book, by the way, and basically to what an awakening journey is all about - learning to prioritize your emotions over your thoughts and to use your emotions wisely to help push you in the right direction.

If you haven't read my other book, this concept of the power of your emotions and why you want to bypass your logical mind as much as possible in order to heal might be a little vague or confusing, but just know for now that your thoughts are actually projections of your feelings and that you want to be connecting to the deepest parts of yourself when doing this reprogramming. Focusing just on the surface layer conscious thoughts is only going to get you so far. You will always find yourself slipping back into old habits if you only work on the conscious level. You need to go deeper and connecting directly to your emotions is how you do this.

I'll explain a bit more about how to do this in a minute...

1C - Expanding the Nature of Triggering Events.

Now you know that you can attach a reminder of some new habit to any event that you encounter in your day-to-day life. That is the core of Mind Hack #1.

"Every time I tie my shoe, I will focus on my breathing and make sure that I'm breathing from my diaphragm".

"Every time I brush my teeth, I will repeat the mantra 'I love myself and I am beautiful'".

"Every time I see a dog, I will remind myself to stand up straight".

Absolutely anything! The idea is to program your brain to connect 2 idea - one idea that represents something that happens in your day to day life, and a second that represents something you want to program into yourself. By connecting these 2 ideas, you have created a subroutine where this external event is helping you embed new programming into your subconscious, to help you grow, heal, and evolve during moments where you used to just be lost in the 3D game of Earth reality. It sounds complicated, but it's simple.

If you're one of those people who likes taking things to extremes, you can be triggering yourself towards self-improvement just about every moment of every day. I wouldn't suggest this, though... because if you overdo it your brain will likely get tired and this will all fade into abstraction. You'll burn yourself out from inner healing and deep reprogramming and give it all up. Plus, you do still need to have SOME focus on your regular life. So, you probably don't want to go that far, but you can install as many subroutines as you like and see where it takes you.

These subroutines don't only need to be tied to random events that the universe will present to you, though. You don't need to wait for these triggering events to present themselves by chance. You can take this Mind Hack even further.

Here are two extra ways that you can trigger subroutines.

First, you can imbue objects with meaning that will keep bringing you back to something. You can buy a piece of jewelry, for example, and before wearing it for the first time - hold it in your hand, look at it, and repeat to yourself out loud what this object means to you and what you want it to remind you of. For example, you could have a bracelet that is there specifically to remind you to stand up straight. All you have to do is focus on this object for a few minutes when you first get it (or you can apply this right now to something you already own and are wearing at this very moment), and repeat the intention that you have about it for a few minutes. Repeat to yourself out loud what subroutine you want to install and - for extra points - allow yourself to feel the positive emotions you will have when you have mastered this new subroutine and the skills and benefits associated with it. Remember, emotions are more powerful than words.

Take a moment to do that right now. Pick something that you are wearing right now. Preferably a piece of jewelry that you wear all the time as opposed to a piece of clothing, but a shirt or whatever you have on will do just fine. If it's a piece of jewelry, take it off and hold it in your hands. Whatever it is, focus on it. Look at it. Think of something you want to remind yourself to do on a regular basis (if you have no ideas right now, I'd recommend choosing a positive mantra that you want to repeat to yourself, and my go-to is always 'I love myself and I am beautiful'), and - with true, positive intent and strong emotion - repeat to yourself what you want this piece of jewelry or clothing to represent to you, for a minute or two.

Once you have done this and you feel like it is solid in your mind, thank your brain for reminding you of it in the future. Thank your brain for always being there for you. Thank it for taking care of you throughout your life, etc. Practice the emotion of gratitude around your brain's ability to work in your favor. Simply take the time out right now to make this a memorable event both consciously and emotionally. Turn this momentary experience into a unique event that sticks out from your day to day routine. A little ritual that is new and interesting to you.

If you do this with full, proper intent and emotion, then the process should be complete. You have created the subconscious association.

If not, you might need to do this consciously a couple of times over the next few days, but soon - and from then on - every time you notice yourself wearing this article of clothing or jewelry you will be brought back to this event and to the emotions tied to it which will trigger this subroutine naturally. The subroutine might not play out EVERY SINGLE TIME you see this object, but the programming will be there and it will happen naturally over and over. Your brain won't be able to resist the association, and you will actively and cheerfully encourage it to do so, so that this pathway becomes more and more ingrained in you every time it happens. You're basically building a positive addiction towards a helpful triggered response.

A second option that you can use to make sure that you play out this subroutine as often as possible is with a simple little dot. Draw a dot on the base of your thumb or somewhere on the back of your hand so that you will see it over and over throughout the day. Every time you notice it will be a reminder for you to focus on whatever it is you wanted to remind yourself of. One of the beautiful aspects of this method is that the meaning of this one can be changed all the time. For a while, this dot on your hand might be a reminder to check your breathing. Then a week later it's a reminder to call your Mom. However you want to use it! It's a very malleable technique.

Your brain is always forming connections. Let's take advantage of this, and tell it what connections you want it to form. It's that simple! Don't underestimate the amount of control you can have over your mind when you put in the conscious effort.

2

Give Your Brain a Cookie

There's a vicious cycle of shame that happens when you are trying to make positive changes in your life and shift a harmful behavior to a beneficial one. You know that you are trying to move from something destructive to something positive, and you instinctively think that your goal is to never have that negative thought, tendency, craving or whatever it is anymore again, immediately. In other words, since you know that you want to change a behavior, you see any instance of that behavior as a failure on your part, and that triggers a shame cycle that is unhelpful.

If you're trying to quit smoking, for example, you know that your goal is to not smoke and to not have the cravings for cigarettes and all that, and so anytime you get a craving or any time that you give in and have a cigarette you believe that you failed and you feel shame around it.

This is a self-perpetuating cycle though, because your habit of smoking is actually a response to uncomfortable emotions in the first place. If you've read Allen Carr's famous book 'Easy Way to Stop Smoking', you'll know that the physical dependence and addiction to smoking isn't actually half as strong as you think it is. The whole reason you are still smoking - even though at least some large part of you knows that you don't want to smoke anymore - is because smoking is one of the ways that you help yourself avoid feeling certain uncomfortable emotions. Stress, overwhelm, worry, guilt, shame, etc. These are all things that make you uneasy, and smoking gives a quick pleasurable nicotine fix and dopamine release that helps cover up that emotional distress that you are otherwise experiencing.

Smoking is - primarily - a method of avoidance and/or soothing for emotional discomfort. It helps you handle uncomfortable emotional situations (albeit in a harmful and ultimately unhelpful way).

So, when you give yourself any shame, doubt or guilt around the things that you are not doing perfectly (while you are in fact trying to change those very behaviors), you reinforce a negative emotional cycle that is going to keep you doing that thing over and over and over again.

To put it simply, if you allow yourself to feel guilty because you smoked, then that feeling of guilt will reinforce your urge to smoke. So, then you'll smoke... and you'll feel guilty... and you'll smoke... and you'll feel guilty, etc. It goes around forever unless you actively take control of it. You need to end this negative shame cycle so that you can actually, and finally, change the behavior that you're ashamed of.

If you focus only on changing the behavior without also changing the emotions, then you will never escape the cycle, but if you focus on changing the emotion first, then you will begin to lessen the urge for the bad behavior altogether, because you don't need to cover up uncomfortable emotions. The goal is for you to confront your guilt and shame first, so that you can feel freer and more comfortable to stop smoking, not to try to eliminate the guilt by ending the bad behavior first. By dealing with the emotion, you will be that much more able to change the behavior – as opposed to the other way around.

You need to begin by focusing on the emotions, which means that you need to end this cycle of guilt and shame you give yourself for 'failing' before you can actually alter your behavior. In order to do this, you will need to shift some beliefs about your bad behavior.

One thing I tell my clients all the time as they move through my 8-week course on Self Love and Shadow Work is that 'so long as you are continuing on your path and making efforts, there is no such thing as failure anymore', and I do mean that quite literally. It's not just some motivational phrase that I use to pump them up and give them strength.

There is NO SUCH THING as failure!!!

Why is there no such thing as failure?

Well, let's take a quick look at how you perceive failure in a situation like this.

First, let's understand and agree that you cannot possibly intentionally change a behavior that you are unaware of. Right? By definition, you can't 'intentionally' do something that you're not consciously aware of and actively choosing, and when it comes to reprogramming subconscious behavior, this reprogramming MUST be done intentionally. You can't change something that you are doing subconsciously without placing conscious attention onto that behavior. It's illogical and impossible.

Let's say that you have a habit of sighing after every time you take a sip of coffee but you've never noticed that before in your life until your spouse points it out to you one day. Now, every time you do it you notice it and you feel weird, strange, uncomfortable, or ashamed and you want to change this behavior. You didn't used to realize that you were doing it, but now you can't help but notice it.

Until your spouse pointed it out to you, it would have been completely impossible for you to make any efforts to change this behavior. You didn't have knowledge of and perspective about the behavior in the first place, so you certainly could not have given it your attention and started making any efforts to change it.

So, you understand that in order to change a behavior and to improve yourself as a human that you need to be able to observe your negative thought patterns and behaviors directly, right?

Great.

Now, recognize that the ONLY possible way that you can even perceive or think that you failed is by noticing and observing negative thought patterns and behaviors. Without moving your conscious attention to this undesired behavior or pattern you could not even possibly recognize a 'failure'. You will only think that you failed when you have decided on a positive behavior you want to practice and when you notice the negative behavior that is taking place instead. The whole thought of 'I failed' is based on you noticing yourself doing something that you don't want to do anymore, or not doing something that you want to do. You think you failed because you observed some behavior that you're trying to change.

There's a paradox here, though. Isn't there?

The ONLY WAY that you can believe that you failed is by noticing a negative pattern that you are trying to change, but - at the same time - the ONLY WAY that you can possibly improve yourself is by noticing that same negative pattern!

In other words, the very first act that you MUST take in order to succeed is also the ONLY act that can possibly make you think that you failed. Noticing a negative behavior is either a failure in your mind (because you just did something you know that you are trying to change), or it is a success because you just observed the thing you are trying to change, which allows you - finally - the opportunity to change it! Whether this was a great success or a disappointing failure is 100% a matter of perspective. You succeeded by noticing old patterns! Noticing them is how you can change them! Yet, you're telling yourself that you failed, which only goes to create a shame cycle that will exacerbate the initial problem. Failure is a mistaken perception about something that was actually a great success!

That means that - on this emotional healing journey - it is literally and logically impossible to fail!

Except, of course... in how you respond to your 'failures'. That is your only test!

If - when you notice yourself performing a behavior that you are trying to change - you get down on yourself and give yourself shame, self-doubt and anger because you think that you failed, then yes... that will perpetuate negative thought cycles and make the situation worse, and we would consider THAT a 'failure'. If, on the other hand, you notice and appreciate that you observed this negative behavior and remind yourself that it is NOT a failure to have that first negative thought, but rather a success to have noticed it, you can escape this shame cycle and actually begin the transformation process.

This is what 'giving the brain a cookie' means.

You need to practice congratulating yourself for noticing bad behavior instead of punishing yourself for having that bad behavior. You need to train your brain to ENJOY the act of noticing old harmful patterns, instead of resenting it. If you remind yourself that noticing these things is actually amazing and that - by noticing them - you are getting better, stronger, happier, and healthier, then your brain will start actively seeking these things out more and noticing them will make you feel better about yourself, rather than worse.

If you know, for example, that you are trying not to resort to anger anymore when someone is rude to you and - instead of yelling and losing control like you used to - to stop and breathe instead, then when you notice yourself getting angry, your goal should be to congratulate yourself in your head for catching it, NOT getting frustrated because you're getting angry.

In a moment, you will get angry. A moment later, you will NOTICE that you got angry, and in THAT very moment is when failure or success will be determined! NOT before. Getting angry initially was NOT a failure, it was just subconscious programming playing out. ONLY once this subconscious pattern reaches your conscious mind will failure or success be determined based on how you react to this observation. If you congratulate yourself in that moment for noticing that you're getting angry, you give your brain a cookie (the reward of positive emotions and self-encouragement) and you allow yourself to change the behavior. Whereas if you get more frustrated with yourself because you still have that subconscious pattern, you will reinforce negative emotions that will reinforce the negative pattern, and ONLY that will be a failure.

All you need to do to succeed is to realize this, and - whenever you notice an unconscious pattern that you are trying to change emerge - literally just think to yourself, "awesome job! I'm so proud of you. Good for you for noticing this behavior and thank you for pointing it out to me". That will give you a sense of pleasure and accomplishment in that moment, giving you extra strength and patience to stop getting angry. It will train your brain to enjoy the experience of catching your old programmed behavior. This sense of accomplishment will release some dopamine and serotonin that will program your brain to want to do this more often. It will associate 'noticing bad behavior' with 'a positive and pleasurable release of endorphins' and it will begin to steer you in this direction more often.

Plus, as I've been saying, noticing bad behavior and responding positively to it is the only way to actually reprogram yourself out of this old cycle altogether. So, if you simply notice your shortcomings and rejoice in noticing them - rather than lament having them in the first place - you are halfway to healing and releasing them.

Shame, on the other hand, will just make the situation worse. Giving yourself crap when you notice these undesired patterns and behaviors will make you feel unpleasant and uncomfortable in that moment, and your brain - in an attempt to protect you from pain - will form defense mechanisms to prevent you from noticing them, thereby sending you deeper and deeper into unconscious auto-pilot mode, and this is basically how you've been living your whole life. You trained yourself to avoid noticing your shortcomings so that you didn't feel the pain and discomfort associated with them, and that kept you going in circles that exacerbated all the problems in your life. You just never noticed.

The moment that you notice the behavior is the fork in that road. In that moment you get to decide if this is going to be a healing moment that makes you better, or just another moment of you running from your pain and piling more trauma on top of the trauma heap that was getting triggered in that moment in the first place. If you choose guilt and shame, then you add another instance of guilt and shame onto the pile and you stay too occupied with that guilt and shame to actually address the inner trigger at all in the moment. Absolutely no healing happens. If, on the other hand, you choose pride and joy about raising your consciousness enough to notice your old behavior, you will have immediately interrupted the old pattern in its tracks and provided yourself an opportunity to consciously choose an alternate reaction.

So, you want to train yourself to 'give your brain a cookie'. You want to reward yourself for catching bad behavior, not guilt yourself for having had it - like you are used to doing. This is a crucial practice of self-love.

Anything that you can think of to reward yourself is good. The simplest way is just to actively and verbally congratulate yourself for noticing this old pattern that used to go unnoticed, but you can certainly take this further. Giving yourself a hug is a good option. If there's a treat that you want to reward yourself with (food or otherwise), that can work. Maybe you can take a minute for a quick dance break to reward yourself and release endorphins. You could choose to give yourself a high five or sing a little song, etc. whatever it is that resonates with you. I generally just stick to congratulating myself in my head, but I wanted to give you some ideas so that you can use whatever feels right to you, and so that you can feel free to brainstorm other ways for yourself.

> Just make sure that you train your brain to realize that having harmful, subconscious behaviors and thought patterns is NOT a failure. Noticing them, on the other hand, is a success.

When you do struggle to maintain a particular goal, be kind and gentle with yourself about it. No more shaming yourself for not being perfect! Eliminate shame and practice gratitude and pride instead and you will reprogram old negative patterns that much more quickly. The positive emotions will push you in the right direction, whereas the negative emotions of guilt and shame move you further away from your goals and further into auto-pilot, fear-based, defense mechanisms that will keep you going on a downward spiral.

There is NO SUCH THING AS FAILURE! So, stop telling yourself that you failed, because doing so will stall your progress. The mere thought that you failed can only be sparked by noticing something that you are trying to change. Noticing it is HOW you change. Therefore, any thought that you failed must have been sparked by a moment which – through a mere shift in perspective – was actually a huge success!

If you think that you failed, it means there was actually a great moment of success there. You just need to realize it!

3

Take Responsibility

When you're learning how to drive, there is a concept called 'defensive driving'. The principle behind it is that you can't trust all the other drivers on the road to do what they are supposed to do. You have to drive defensively to make room for error on behalf of other drivers, instead of just driving on ahead thinking that 'so long as I am following the rules, I'm safe, because everyone else will follow the rules too'.

This is a principle that we sorely need to adopt in all the other areas of our lives as well if we want to grow, evolve, and heal. Until we learn to take full responsibility for our actions, feelings, and circumstances instead of trying to blame all those around us, we will forever be stuck in a victim mentality that prevents us from ever being truly in control of our lives. We concede powerlessness to the world by staying in that mentality. We surrender to a nasty situation that doesn't actually need to be, and we convince ourselves that that's just the way it is.

This whole inner healing process, though, is about claiming your power back; from yourself, from your unconscious mind, and from the world. To reclaim your sovereignty by consciously and intentionally choosing the energy and emotion with which you respond to whatever the world throws at you.

The more that you are able to remain calm, unafraid, and in control of yourself when things aren't going how you planned, the more able you will be to act in a manner that doesn't make the situation worse, and that allows you to turn an unpleasant moment of emotional distress into an instance of healing and growth that can make your life better, instead of a moment of acting defensively from an emotion of fear in a way that will make your life worse.

You need to start noticing all the ways in which you yourself are helping to perpetuate negative cycles in your life. If you don't, and if you keep on blaming others instead, then you will never take control of your life and will never be able to improve it.

> **The way that I like to express this is;**
>
> **It may not be true that everything happens for a reason, but if you choose to learn and grow from the bad things, then they WILL HAVE HAPPENED for a reason.**

You give meaning to the unpleasant things in your life by learning and growing from them. A failure is only a failure if you let it keep you down or if you don't learn anything from it. If you DO learn something from it, then this unpleasant experience was simply a necessary step on the road to success, not an actual failure. All of your failures are actually just challenges trying to push you in the direction of greatness, and basically all great men (and women) have said and agreed that what separates the winners from the losers is how they deal with failure.

This leads us to a giant lesson that we need to truly accept and embody in our lives: Everything is happening FOR us, not to us.

Everything is a lesson pushing us in the right direction of where we are supposed to be.

To put it another way, every moment of emotional distress that you experience is pointing you in the direction of where you need healing.

I'm going to say that again, because this needs to be hammered in!

EVERY moment of emotional distress is pointing you in the direction of where you need healing! Except in the rare moments of legitimate, life threatening danger and victimization, all of your day-to-day moments of emotional discomfort are only uncomfortable because they are triggering something inside of you that you haven't dealt with, and that is a clue towards your own liberation and greatest version. It is an opportunity to heal.

If you didn't need healing around the very thing that triggered you, then it would NOT have triggered you in the first place. It's just that simple. It only hurts because there is already a wound there, not because of the actual thing that happened.

So, the question then becomes; which element of this unpleasant experience do you think you should turn your attention to? The thing that triggered you (the thing outside of you that you can't control), or the thing that got triggered (the issue inside of you that you CAN control)? Which choice do you think is more likely to give you real results and a sense of inner peace?

When you look at things this way, you can start to see that every time you get triggered into anger, fear, guilt, shame, etc... is actually a clue as to what wounds you still carry inside of you. It's happening FOR you - to help you improve yourself and your life - not TO you - to make you a victim. The choice of how to see and react to this experience is up to you, though. You can choose to follow the clues of this unpleasant triggering experience to push you towards growth and inner healing, or you can keep focusing on the outside world and the person that did you wrong that just triggered you. You can see this as a learning and growing experience for yourself and for your own benefit because you are in control of your life, or you can view it as just another instance of you being victimized by the world around you.

One belief and reaction empowers you, while the other one convinces you to just concede defeat to the world and to wallow in your own self-pity.

The victim mentality allows you to stay in your comfort zone and to avoid taking any responsibility for your life. This helps you avoid some small form of emotional discomfort in the moment, but it is also this mentality that has kept you from progressing in your life and that is keeping you stuck in old, negative, self-harming cycles. By avoiding the momentary emotional discomfort, you create a negative cycle of pain and disappointment in your life. In other words, by trying to avoid fleeting pain in the moment (by ignoring your own wounds and instead focusing on the person that hurt you) you create a life full of lasting pain for yourself.

It's a toss-up between short term pain and long term pain. Are you going to confront the emotional discomfort inside of you in the moment so that you can heal it and release it, or are you going to focus on the thing that hurt you so that you don't need to confront the uncomfortable emotion that this brought up, and thereby perpetuate a cycle of self-loathing that will just have you continually getting triggered again and again?

The more that you can choose to see everything as happening FOR you, the more able you will be to turn every moment of emotional distress into a moment of healing, instead of a moment of piling more trauma on top of the heap of unresolved emotions that is already living and getting triggered inside of you.

EVERY moment of emotional distress and getting triggered ends up one of two ways - either you use that moment as an opportunity to release the past pain inside of you that is getting triggered, or you avoid your emotions one more time, and store up the extra instance of that emotion that just got triggered in the moment. In that case, the pile of unresolved emotions in you gets bigger, just waiting for the next trigger.

You want to train yourself to always be looking inside of yourself for answers and to constantly try to face your own uncomfortable emotions and thoughts, rather than putting the blame onto the outside world or ignoring the role that you are playing in creating the situation. You want to take full control of your life, and that will mean taking full responsibility for everything that you think and feel and all of your emotional reactions to what the world throws at you. You no longer want to accept the reasoning of 'this was someone else's fault' in your life, because that takes away your power to change things.

Stop blaming others! Take control! Accept FULL responsibility!

The 'mind hack' here, then, is - as often as you can remember to do so - to continuously ask yourself the following question:

'Even when someone else is genuinely at fault, what could I have done to change the situation?'[1]

It's not about judgment or blame anymore. It doesn't matter who's at fault, or who was right and who was wrong. There's no point or benefit in engaging in that debate. It's just about outcome and consequences. Which would you rather? To be justified in blaming and getting angry at someone who did you wrong and to be able to

[1] I want to re-iterate here that what I'm proposing is NOT a form of 'victim-blaming'. I am NOT saying that you are at fault for all the terrible things that have happened to you and for the big moments of trauma and victimization that you may have experienced in this life. I am merely saying that a shift in perspective about how we react to our regular, day-to-day problems will help us take more control over our lives, and help us become victimized less often, because we no longer put our lives into other people's hands in the same way. DO NOT retroactively apply this reasoning to the worst moments of trauma in your life. Just start learning to take responsibility for your life as it is right now, so that you can start moving more in the right direction.

judge them for it - but thereby train yourself to be the victim of your circumstances, incapable of changing your future? Or, to not feel the need to complain and judge, because you've handled the situation in the best way possible, avoided most of the damage, and learned from the whole thing?

Most people are actually choosing option 'A' every day, not realizing that they are choosing it and not realizing just how much they are actually allowing themselves to revel and bask in the judgment and anger that they are feeling towards the other person in the situation. I get this a lot with clients. I try to explain to them the subconscious reasoning behind their reactions to challenges in their lives, and their response is often to try to explain to me why they are JUSTIFIED in getting angry in that situation.

My response is always the same: "Yes. You are correct. From a 3D, human, morality and ethics perspective, you are right. The other person was hurtful, and you are 'justified' in getting angry. But... What do you want for yourself? Do you want to **justify** your anger, or **overcome** it? Justifying your anger is actually just defending your own pain. You're trying to convince yourself (and others) why you SHOULD stay in pain and why you're allowed to be, and I'm trying to show you that you don't have to be in pain anymore. It's your choice!"

It's certainly a lot easier to judge and get angry at others than it is to take responsibility for the emotions being triggered in you because that means that you don't need to recognize your role in the whole thing. It means that you get to see the other person as the villain and you as the poor and helpless victim that could not have possibly done anything to avoid what happened. It's a very unpleasant and unhelpful mentality... but it's easy.

So, again... ask yourself "even when someone else is genuinely at fault, what could I have done differently to have prevented this?"

When you start asking yourself this question more and more, you will start realizing how many uncomfortable triggered emotions you were actually running from by allowing yourself to get angry and judgmental instead of introspective. It will start opening up a lot of realizations to you about how fear and anger were actually controlling you this whole time. It was never about logic, rationality, ethics and social etiquette like you thought it was. It was always just about fear and defensiveness. You will recognize how your outwards reaction of anger was actually based on an unwillingness to look at your own role in creating this event as well as the uncomfortable emotions that got triggered in you, and you will start to see how much more in control of your life you could be when you stop blaming others for what isn't working out in your favor.

Learn to take responsibility, and you will learn to start releasing fear.

4

Affirmation Hacks

Let's talk about affirmations for a bit and ways that you can increase their effectiveness, but first - for those of you who aren't already aware - what are affirmations?

You can basically think of affirmations as mantras. In fact, I find it hard to find a strict way of distinguishing between the two. They're basically the same thing. They are simple phrases that you repeat to yourself in order to help you relax, gain strength or convince your mind of something.

Like meditation and other pseudo-spiritual practices, affirmations are something that most of the Western world thought was pretty hokey, spiritual or overly 'touchy-feely' 20 years ago. It was the type of thing that people would laugh at you for if they caught you using them freely. Surely, some people still feel that way, but it's become more obvious, accepted and common to use affirmations as a practice to help you program your brain for positivity and success.

How do affirmations work?

Think of your brain like a wide open, unspoiled, fresh field of grass. If you walk through a field once, you'll barely leave a mark. But if you walk through it 10 times, 100 times, 10,000 times... eventually you start paving a clear pathway. Eventually, you'll pave a pathway so clear that you would never even think to walk any other way through the field again. You will always naturally gravitate to the path of least resistance, the same way that water always flows to the lowest point.

Keep walking that pathway long enough and eventually you'll completely forget that you were the one who paved that pathway in the first place, that the pathway could have been completely different, and that you can choose to start walking down a new pathway any time you want to.

You've spent your lifetime paving certain pathways in your brain, creating conscious and subconscious beliefs about yourself and the world, thereby determining your personality, disposition, attitude, and all the ways in which you interact with yourself and others. It is these subconscious beliefs that make you act in certain ways and that lead you to choose one path over another in your life. These subconscious beliefs that you have unknowingly paved are secretly in control of everything that's been going on in your life and - perhaps until this very moment - you had no idea that this was happening.

You haven't realized or recognized the fact that you have been programming your brain every second of every day. Every time you think a thought, perform an action, experience an event, watch a TV show, or read a book like this one you are firing neurons down certain pathways in your brain and every time you fire neurons down a certain pathway you help to pave that pathway, training your brain to go down that same pathway again next time, especially in moments when you're not paying a whole lot of attention. Since you never realized that this was happening, you never did pay attention to how you were programming your brain and you passively allowed a lot of negative and self-harming pathways to be deeply and solidly paved into your mind.

Your whole life you have allowed the programming of your brain to happen TO you. You have been passive in this process of training your brain. You could have actively chosen how you wanted to program yourself, but you never realized that this was an option so you sat back and let the programming just happen on its own. It's like you've been a fish asleep in the ocean, letting the current take you wherever it wanted to go, never realizing that you have the ability to swim in any direction you want to if you just wake up and put in some effort!

Your goal now - in this healing journey that you are on - is to start actively taking control of how your brain is being programmed, and affirmations are one of the ways that you begin to do this. The fact that your brain is constantly being programmed is actually an amazing gift that you can use to make your life better, but if you don't take control of it and do that actively, then the world programs your brain for you, and let's face it... our society is not equipped to train our brains for positivity, love, and success. The modern world programs us for fear, desire and attachment.

Affirmations are not magic, nor are they spiritual 'woo-woo' nonsense. They are simply a method of actively choosing which pathways you want to pave in your brain so that you can slowly shift from fear-based programming to love based programming. It's basic psychology and neuro-biology. Your brain is constantly forming connections, and you want to take control of what connections and associations you are forming at any given moment.

As you begin to use affirmations to train your brain, please do keep in mind that change cannot happen instantly. You have spent a lifetime paving the old pathways. You've thought to yourself "I'm unattractive" 100,000 times in your life. So, it's going to be a while before your brain can be genuinely reprogrammed to "I know that I'm beautiful", just by saying it over and over.

You need to pave the new pathway more deeply than the first one that you've already paved, so that when you get triggered and your brain switches into auto-pilot mode, the new pathway of "I love myself and I am beautiful" is the natural pathway for the neurons to flow through. If you walked down the old pathway 100,000 times, then you are going to need to walk down the new pathway 100,000 times before it becomes as natural as the old pathway once was. So, be patient with yourself as you work through this reprogramming.

Fortunately, with these mind hacks and other healing techniques we are using, the reprogramming will actually happen much more quickly than that. It took you a lifetime to pave the old pathways by allowing it to happen passively, and you are learning how to repave the new ones exponentially more quickly by doing it consciously (and with advanced techniques), but still... it's going to take some time, so be patient with yourself.

To recap; what is an affirmation? It is a phrase that you repeat to yourself in order to consciously fire neurons down a certain pathway to create new connections and associations in your brain that will help reprogram you out of fear, guilt, and shame and into love, joy and compassion. It is a simple way of training your brain to believe something by actively choosing to reinforce the thought around that belief as often as possible. After all, a belief is merely a thought that you keep thinking and that you find yourself incapable of not thinking. So, you want to actively start choosing which thoughts you are going to keep thinking at the conscious level, so that these new thoughts can become ingrained in you at the subconscious level.

Now that you know what they are, how they work, and what the goal is, let's talk about a few tricks that you can use to increase the speed at which you pave these new pathways in your brain with affirmations.

A - It's NOT about the words!

The first thing to understand is that the pathways you have paved in your brain are not based on 'language'. It is not the words themselves that are the content of these pathways. Words are just symbols that are meant to represent and express an idea, concept, desire, emotion, etc. They are representational. The words could change while the content remains the same, and vice versa.

Your subconscious mind doesn't operate on language. It operates on frequency. The words that you think (or hear) consciously in your head, carry with them a particular frequency of the emotions, intentions and meanings that are behind them. The very same words used in two different contexts can have completely different emotions behind them. In the most obvious example, you might be saying something sarcastically, where the words "thank you so much!" could carry with them either the emotions of true gratitude and appreciation or the emotions of judgment and frustration.

So, since it's not the words themselves that are the important factor here, if you're using affirmations and all you're doing is repeating the words in your head over and over mindlessly and with no true intention or focus around them, then they really aren't going to have much of an impact. The language is just the surface layer of their meaning and if you want to truly reprogram your brain then you are going to need to dive deeper.

The goal with affirmations, then, is actually to use them to PRACTICE a feeling.

If your affirmation is, for example, "I am beautiful", the whole point is to first focus on what it would feel like to truly believe that you are beautiful. Try to connect with that confidence and that feeling of freedom and relaxation that you would have if you knew that you were beautiful and if you were therefore less self-conscious about your looks and that much more able to enjoy every moment of every day.

Every moment that you are able to tap into that feeling inside of yourself and to truly focus on it, you are shooting neurons down the positive subconscious pathways of self-love, assurance and confidence; and you are paving those neural-pathways at a much deeper level than if you were to just say the words. Emotions are a deeper and more fundamental part of your psyche than your surface layer conscious thoughts. The words of an affirmation are meant to help you trigger the emotion associated with the thought, so that you can practice feeling it and connecting with it. For one brief moment (or... for as many moments as you practice this) you are interrupting the old negative thought cycles that your fear-based emotions have paved throughout the years and you are practicing and paving the positive cycles that you want to move towards instead.

Do this enough times and with enough passion, emotion, and intention - and those new pathways will become the norm for you.

So, think of your affirmations like Peter Pan's happy thought. In order to fly he needed to have one happy thought in mind and focus on it, but the thought could have been anything and it could have changed from day to day. It didn't matter at all what the content of the thought was. It only mattered that it filled him with pure happiness. It was the emotion that he needed in order to fly, not the thought itself.

Remember... use your affirmations to help you practice an emotion because every moment that you stay in that emotion helps program your brain to revert back to that emotion later on. The language-based content of the thought doesn't matter half as much as the emotion that is associated with it. Ultimately, you won't even need the affirmations themselves once you learn how to just practice being in the vibration of love, joy, or bliss. The words of the affirmation are just an entry point to the deeper meaning and practice and are relatively meaningless in and of themselves.

If you don't believe the affirmations, they won't work, and you must feel them to believe them. Connect to the emotions that the words are meant to exemplify.

B - Add Melody

Another thing that you can do to increase the efficiency of your affirmations is to add melody to them, and/or to actually sing them.

Adding a melody can help in a few ways.

Firstly, the melody itself carries with it a particular emotion. There are happy melodies and sad melodies. The relationships between the notes used in the melodies carry with them a certain power. Music has an effect on us that goes far beyond the logical, conscious mind. There are timeless pieces of music that can evoke a deep emotional response from people of all ages, races, and genders. You could probably go back to the cavemen and play them 'Hey Jude' or Beethovens 'Moonlight Sonata' and even they would be touched by it.

Adding a happy melody to the words that you are using to program something into yourself evokes an emotion that amplifies the impact of the words in that moment. If your goal is to program your subconscious mind at layers that go beyond rational cognition, then music is an excellent way to help you go deeper. The melody will help the words you are using reach a deeper layer of your unconscious mind and help you pave a new pathway more quickly and efficiently.

Secondly, the melody makes the affirmation more memorable to your conscious mind. It becomes a bit of an earworm that repeats itself in your head over and over, all day long. The melody will trick your brain into repeating the words and the programming even when you are not paying specific attention to it. The words and the melody will often be playing in the background of your mind while you go about your daily business, and this will help you program this new belief into yourself - even when you're not doing it intentionally.

Thirdly, the act of singing is itself much more powerful than the act of speaking. It naturally uses more energy, more parts of your body and gets your brain and your heart more automatically involved in the activity. Singing is a very powerful way to help connect your head to your heart and your mind to your body, not to mention that engaging in musical practices unites many different areas of your brain. Music requires parts of your brain responsible for processing information, for creativity, for muscle memory, for emotion etc. Creating music helps engage many areas of your brain at once which helps you form deeper associations in the moment. The more parts of your brain that are active in a given moment, the more deeply you are forming connections.

So, whether you love your voice or not, sing those affirmations loud! And have fun with it! The singing and the emotion will help accelerate the paving of these new pathways immensely.

C - Switch Languages

This is just a quick little trick for those of you who happen to speak more than one language.

Whatever your primary language is these days, consider doing your affirmations in another language from time to time.

Once again, this helps you bypass the conscious mind a bit and activate multiple parts of your brain at once. In order for you to process words in a secondary language there is a translation process that needs to happen subconsciously in your mind. It's more of an active process than listening to your primary language.

Also, if you're not paying a lot of attention, your conscious mind is more likely to zone out when you're listening to a secondary language and since your goal is to bypass the conscious mind and get down to the subconscious, this can be helpful at times. You can repeat an affirmation in a secondary language so that your conscious mind is a little more distracted while you continue to repeat it. Your subconscious mind - on the other hand - catches everything, and keeping your conscious mind out of it helps the words have a deeper impact on the unconscious parts of yourself.

5

Stop Saying That!

In the last section, we were using affirmations to take control of what pathways we are actively paving in our brains. We were making sure that - as often as possible - the things that we actively think and say are helping to program us for positivity. Now, we need to deal with the flip side of that coin. We need to make sure that we **stop** paving negative pathways in our brains as much as possible. Otherwise, the positive work that we've been doing is going to be cancelled out by all the negative stuff that we think and say when we are not paying attention.

If you spend half your day consciously repeating the positive affirmation of "I love myself and I am beautiful" but then spend the rest of the day thinking "ugh... everything is terrible and I'm never going to accomplish anything", then you're not really going to make much lasting progress, are you? So, now you need to turn your attention to the negative pathways that you are slipping into, and actively try to prevent yourself from reinforcing them.

This is generally going to prove to be a little more difficult because you first need to train yourself to notice and catch the negative thought cycles before you can start actively taking control

45

of them. You need to actively notice and recognize the self-harming patterns you are in **while** you are having them, and that takes a fair amount of self-awareness, patience, and emotional strength. It does seem more difficult than just thinking "I want to think positive things as often as possible", but really... when you understand what's going on in your head that is creating these cycles and just start putting your attention to that a little bit, you'll find that interrupting old negative thought patterns is easier than you think.

The first thing that you need to do is to understand the subconscious cycles that have been happening inside of you which have been creating these negative thought patterns in the first place.

Your head, your heart, and your gut (your thoughts, emotions, and sensations) are constantly operating in tandem to create your experience of reality and thereby to push you in a given direction, but you have been living exclusively from your head, very disconnected from the intuitive and instinctive parts of yourself that are operating beneath the surface. As a result of this, you have never been able to truly notice how the things you THOUGHT you were actively controlling and choosing based on logic in your head were actually just knee-jerk reflexes to other emotions and sensations that have been happening. You believed that you were acting according to rational and justified logic, but your brain was really just deluding you into thinking that it was in control. It was never in control. It was always responding to your emotions. You just never realized it because you were still stuck in that old programming, unable to view it all from a higher perspective.

Marketers and salespeople all over the world know very well that people don't actually make their buying decisions based on logic. They make the decision based on emotion first, and they use logic to justify it later. Ask anyone who has spent years in sales and they will tell you this. Well, what makes you think that any other area of your life is any different? They're not. In every area of our lives, we make decisions based on emotions first, and then justify those decisions logically after the fact. This just happens so quickly and so subtly that it's easy to ignore and miss.

It's important that you start noticing that all the logical reasons that you thought were 'justified' when you made judgments about a person or situation had nothing to do with logic at all, but were actually emotional responses to external triggers. Your brain just tries to justify its emotional response afterwards so that you can pretend to be in alignment with yourself. It is doing its best to avoid any extra inner conflict in you, and so it puts itself into alignment with the decision that your heart just pushed you to make by convincing you that there are good logical reasons behind it.

Simply put, you were actually responding to an uncomfortable emotion in your heart, not to logic, but your brain doesn't like that. Your brain wants to think that it is in control and that it is justified in the decisions that you made. So, it creates logical reasoning around an emotional decision, so that you can feel as if you were justified in your reaction. You are justifying your pain, instead of introspectively noticing it so that you can heal it. This is a defense mechanism. It is a way that you can avoid having to notice inner conflict and an emotional reaction.

When you are acting from love, this is extremely beneficial and is basically what you are trying to attain through your healing journey - to get your brain into alignment with a heart that is acting based on love. You WANT to be able to convince your brain that an emotional decision was the right one - when the root emotion was love. That is what learning to trust your intuition is all about.

But when you are getting triggered - making decisions based on fear - and your head aligns itself with those decisions in order to 'protect you' from the instantaneous discomfort of that negative emotion, this creates a cycle that makes everything worse. You acted poorly because of an undesired emotional reaction, which makes you feel worse, so you make worse decisions, which leads to worse outcomes, which leads to worse feelings and worse decisions, etc. Around and around you go.

Ok... so... what exactly is the source or the nature of this cycle? Why are you allowing your brain to defensively justify your pain, rather than learning how to feel it and release it?

Basically, this cycle began whenever you first started experiencing trauma. Something in your reality created an uncomfortable emotion that - in the moment - you didn't know how to deal with and you weren't safe to deal with it. For example, the initial trauma might have been something as simple as getting scolded by your parents. In that moment you needed to release certain emotions, but also in that moment you knew that if you were to cry more or shout or express what needed to be expressed that it would lead to you being punished or rejected even more. Expressing yourself and your pain would have led to more pain in that moment when you were already feeling unsafe, exposed, vulnerable, and in danger.

So, your brain created this defense mechanism. It closed itself off to the emotions that you were feeling in that moment and took charge of the situation by trying to force you to adapt your behavior to the circumstances of the outside world. It trained you to push away the deep part of yourself that was hurting in that moment and to just try and survive the storm.

In moments of genuine trauma, this was in fact the best thing to do. You weren't safe. You needed to survive. You needed to make it through the storm so that you could regroup and get yourself on solid footing again.

The problem is that when the storm cleared you never actually took the time to release the emotion that was created in that moment. It's like you told yourself, "I'll deal with this later when I'm safe", but you just never came back to deal with it. So, it's stuck inside of you. You kept on piling more issues onto the heap, telling yourself that you would deal with it later, and then you pretended like nothing happened. So, all that stuff that you put aside to be 'dealt with later' is still there, dragging you down, and you don't want to look at it because it's uncomfortable.

Now, when something happens in the world that is not truly a big deal but resonates with some of the pain that's trapped inside of you, it brings up all of the past pain of the same frequency that you have put aside to be dealt with 'later'. This is a 'trigger'. Some event that resonates with a certain kind of past pain. A small instance of anger makes you feel all of your repressed anger. A small instance of jealousy makes you feel all of your past jealousy. The current situation creates a small emotion that connects you to the whole reservoir of that same trapped emotion inside of you.

As I've mentioned though, this is actually happening for your benefit. Your brain, your heart and your gut are trying to help you by bringing to your attention all of those things that you promised yourself you would deal with but never did. This is your emotional body trying to do its job by forcing you to confront all of the things that are holding you back.

The problem, however, is that your brain still thinks that you are in danger. Since it is still holding on to this pain from the past and since you have not yet raised your consciousness high enough to notice these old cycles, your brain continues to operate as if you are still in the same danger that you were in when this initial trauma happened. It is still trying to protect you from a threat that is no longer present because it is still holding on that old unresolved fear.

So, when the past pain comes up because your emotional body is trying to get you to deal with it, your brain shifts into 'problem-solving' mode and tries to protect you by pushing away this uncomfortable sensation and emotion because - presuming you are still in danger - allowing yourself to feel this right now would put you in more danger, as it was when you first experienced the trauma. Your brain is acting as if there is a threat right now and it turns its

49

attention to the outside world and to whatever external problem just triggered you, in an attempt to solve 'the problem', even though the only real problem was the emotion that got triggered inside of you. Your brain is trying to protect you, but since there's nothing external to actually protect you from in that moment, it focuses on the entirely wrong issue, thereby perpetuating a negative fear-based cycle.

You then proceed to make a decision or to go down a train of thought that was sparked entirely by an emotion that you don't want to feel, and you convince yourself that this was 'logically and rationally justified'. So, you think that you are responding to a legitimate situation outside of yourself, but you are really only responding to an uncomfortable and unresolved emotion inside of you that was trying to express itself in that moment FOR YOUR BENEFIT, but that you still continue to ignore because you are afraid and think that you're in danger.

In other words, you convinced yourself that your decision was logical and that it didn't come from an emotion, when in reality, your decision came from a **desperate need to avoid an emotion** and - in that sense - **the emotion that you were trying to avoid was in fact the ultimate decision-making factor**. The emotion was actually in control of your decision after all, because you made your choice entirely based on the reasoning of 'how to not feel that emotion'.

The important take-away here is that the conscious thoughts that are popping up in your head at any given moment are actually a byproduct of whatever emotions you are either allowing or not allowing yourself to feel in that moment. For Mind Hack #5, then, you are going to start turning your attention to the feelings that come along with these thoughts, and when you notice thoughts that are connected to negative emotions (when you have thoughts that don't feel good or that reinforce negative beliefs), you are going to interrupt and change them as quickly as possible. You are going to make sure that you do not allow your brain to program itself for fear and negativity, by consciously and actively interrupting thought patterns that are based on fear and emotional avoidance.

A - Watch Your Words

Let's start off as generally as possible.

Let's say that you just got into a fight with your partner and they are making you feel bad about something, and let's say that you've been spending the day walking around thinking to yourself "that bitch" or "that jerk". What do you think is the emotion behind thoughts like that? What frequency do you think those thoughts carry with them, and what frequency and emotion do you think that you are allowing yourself to program into your brain every single time you think those words?

You might be thinking that having those thoughts running around your head is a 'legitimate' and 'logic based' response to whatever it is that your partner did, but hopefully by now you're starting to recognize that it's actually an emotional response. It has nothing to do directly with the situation of what happened, it has to do with the insecure and uncomfortable emotion that is being triggered inside of you. Allowing this emotional response to continue in your head and to continue guiding your thoughts and your reasoning is certainly not going to lead to any positive outcomes, will it?

Allowing yourself to think these thoughts will have a few effects. Firstly, it will cultivate and reinforce the energy and emotions of judgment, resentment, anger, blame, etc. All of these are negative emotional frequencies that - cultivated in you - just push you more towards being a bitter, angry, and resentful person. These emotions simply don't feel good. Secondly, these thoughts will encourage more separation between you and your partner. They are 'adversarial' kinds of thoughts, where it's you against them, and you are right where they are wrong. These thoughts are only going to breed more resentment, more bitterness, and further arguments between the two of you. Thirdly, your brain is going to try to justify and rationalize these emotionally based thoughts, and will invent more reasons to be upset at your partner, thereby driving you even further into resentment and anger.

This is all an illusion of your brain, trying to make sense of an emotionally charged reaction that is actually based in past trauma, not your current experience.

This is uncomfortable, unpleasant, and unhelpful, but you have been allowing yourself to go down this road over and over because it has been easier than focusing inwards and recognizing your own pain and shortcomings. It is easier to blame others, to blame the outside world, and to justify your own pain and bad behavior than it is to notice it, feel it, and take control of it.

The best option for a positive outcome would be to remain calm, to master yourself and your reactions, and to have a loving conversation with your partner about what happened. Even in the worst of cases where whatever problem you're dealing can't be reconciled, the best thing for you would be to learn how NOT to get angry, but how to walk away instead and put up healthy boundaries, based on an emotion of unconditional self-love.

The emotional reaction based in fear, insecurity, and defensiveness is not going to help anything at all, nor is it going to feel good, and you need to recognize here that walking around all day saying "that bitch" in your head is cultivating those fear-based defense mechanisms and the uncomfortable and unhelpful emotions that you are trying to work through. Allowing yourself to think these thoughts is your way of avoiding feeling an uncomfortable emotion about yourself and your past, and it is reinforcing these negative cycles that are going to keep you in pain and sabotaging your relationship and your life.

And yet... you tell yourself that it's a logical, natural, and justified reaction. You tell yourself that the bad behavior of another means that you are **justified** in feeling this way and in being angry with the other person, when really, it's just because you're insecure and in pain and don't know how to feel that or express it. In fact, from a human perspective... sure... you ARE 'justified' in feeling anger and resentment towards this person, but from a higher perspective you should ask yourself, 'which would you rather... to justify your pain or to heal from it?'

STOP TRYING TO JUSTIFY YOUR PAIN!

It's only going to keep you going in circles. Do not CHOOSE to rationalize a reason to make it ok for you to be angry. Instead, notice your actions, words, and thoughts that are being sparked by anger and choose to interrupt and change them because **you don't want to feel angry anymore**. It's not about the morality and ethics of what you're saying about the other person. It's just about self-love! You don't want to keep feeling angry. You don't want to keep sabotaging your life with emotional reactions. Screw ethics... this is about self-love and inner peace.

So, when you're walking around all day thinking to yourself "that jerk", you are actually allowing a subconscious cycle starting from the heart to dictate your whole perception of an event that probably wasn't such a huge deal in the first place, and by allowing that anger cycle to go unnoticed, you act on it, and you allow it to repeat itself over and over. Thinking "that jerk" because you believe you are justified in being angry will just keep you angry and will make any bad situation you are in worse by causing you to act based on that anger.

One of the first steps to fixing your emotional reactions then, will be to take control of the conscious thoughts that are based in negative emotional defense mechanisms.

So, you need to start being very mindful of all the thoughts that you have. You don't want to cultivate thoughts of judgment, anger, blame, etc. Start recognizing that any thoughts that you have like this are actually causing YOU harm. Allowing yourself to justify your pain and to blame others and think these negative thoughts about other people is causing YOU harm! It's not that 'you have to refrain from saying bad things about other people because it's rude or wrong'. It's about energy, emotion, and - dare I say it - a higher truth. It's about the basic facts regarding your emotions, the ways that you are training your brain, and what reactions and responses are in your own best interests.

That's kind of the ironic beauty of what you're working on here. Most people think that you want to stop having these angry and judgmental thoughts out of some moral or ethical responsibility to the other person (or maybe to God, for the religious amongst you), when ACTUALLY it is just because you are doing what is best for you. YOU don't want to feel the pain of these cycles of judgment and blame anymore. It's just not worth it for you to carry that negative energy. You are finally starting to wake up enough to notice that this is happening and now that you notice that it's happening, don't you want to start taking control of it?

It is because YOU are tired of feeling this way that you are going to turn your attention to these things. You don't owe it to anybody other than yourself. You are just starting to recognize - hopefully, by now - that you (and your avoidance of your unresolved emotions) are at the center of all of your suffering, and you're tired of it. You are no longer going to allow other people's pain and bad behavior to turn into YOUR pain and bad behavior. You are going to stop letting the world make you bitter and angry because YOU are tired of being bitter and angry, and because you are finally ready to rise above this cycle and to start taking control of your life.

It's a mentality of "screw other people... I'm going to be kind to them for ME!" It's an ironic and amusing paradox, for sure. You are going to be unfathomably kind to others because you care about yourself, NOT because you care about them!

I mean... obviously you do care about other people. I'm just saying that self-love is the foundation.

Any time that you encounter negative thoughts - that you now notice and understand are coming from pain, defensiveness, and insecurity - you are going to actively turn your attention towards them and start focusing on them directly because you are now at a high enough state of consciousness and self-awareness to recognize the damage that these negative thoughts are having on your psyche, on your emotional well-being, and on your life through your fear based, defensive reactions. You are going to recognize these thought patterns, as well as the unhelpful and unpleasant emotions behind them, and start taking action to replace these old unconscious self-harming defense mechanisms with introspective, healing processes that are going to push you in the direction of your own growth and evolution.

Here is what you are going to do from here on out when you notice yourself slipping into negative and judgmental thought processes:

Firstly, go back to Mind Hack #2 that we spoke of in this book - *Give Your Brain a Cookie.*

You want to make sure that you train your brain to enjoy and appreciate noticing these negative thought cycles, rather than feeling pain, guilt, and shame because you had them. It is NOT a failure that you had these negative thoughts, it is a SUCCESS that you noticed them! You didn't notice them in the past - not from an observer's point of view, at least. They've been happening for years, you just never realized it and that is why you have kept going in circles. So, don't beat yourself up for having had these negative thoughts in the moment. Congratulate yourself for noticing them, because that is the necessary first step towards healing and becoming a better version of you. Good for you!

Secondly, you are going to replace the negative thought that you just had with the positive opposite of it at least three times. If, for example, you noticed yourself thinking "that jerk", you will stop and notice it, congratulate yourself for interrupting the old thought pattern (by having noticed it you immediately rerouted your thoughts), and then repeat something like "this person is beautiful and I love them, and they only acted this way because they are in pain, just like I am". You want to replace the divisive thought and belief with one based on compassion and understanding. Or, if you were walking around thinking "I'm so cursed, everything is always terrible for me", then you would stop and reverse that into "I know that I'm held guided and protected every step of the way".

If, every time you notice a negative thought, you congratulate yourself and reinforce the opposite positive thought three times, that means that you are constantly putting more active programming into your love-based thoughts and beliefs than the negative ones, instead of allowing the old cycle of negative thoughts to keep piling on top of themselves and amplifying each other. You are slowly starting to pave deeper pathways of positivity than the pre-paved ones of negativity.

Every time that you notice a negative thought and replace it three times with a positive one, you are cultivating a 3:1 ratio of positive versus negative thinking in your brain, and this will slowly start shifting you towards an overall positive programming of your mind. It will take time for you to pave these new pathways so that they are more deeply ingrained than the old negative ones, but this reprogramming can be simple and easy by just observing the negative thought cycles and replacing them with positive ones at the conscious level.

Now, true healing needs to be done below that conscious, language-based level. You need to connect directly to your emotions and let them run through you. But this is step #1 to no longer running from and ignoring these uncomfortable emotions, so that you can begin working on the deeper issues - which you couldn't have done before you noticed and interrupted the old thought patterns.

> Recognize the self-harming nature of allowing yourself to think negative and judgmental thoughts about others, so that you can turn your attention back to what is happening inside of yourself at the emotional level. This is the only way to start expanding and growing.

B - Stop Trying to Explain Yourself.

Why do you think we spend so much of our time trying to explain ourselves and our beliefs to others? We do this a lot. We get into arguments and debates about the things that we believe, trying to force others to understand them or agree with them, and we tend to convince ourselves that we are doing this for a 'real' reason, maybe because that thing that we believe is so fundamental and important that the other person NEEDS to believe it too. We convince ourselves that it is an act of altruism or of moral obligation to convince this other person of something that we believe.

If you are being true to yourself though, ask yourself... the vast majority of the time that you are trying to convince someone of something, has it been because you are truly trying to share your love, light and brilliance with others, or has it been because some part of you is seeking validation about your own thoughts and beliefs? Have you been chasing approval and trying to impress people? Or have you maybe been trying to force others to see what you see and believe what you believe to help you avoid some pain of confusion and inner conflict inside of you, either about that thing that you believe or about the discomfort of not having your beliefs validated by others (which is actually just triggering some old pain inside of you from past trauma of not being respected, validated, or accepted)?

If you're not sure what the answer to that question is, then just ask yourself; 'How many times have I allowed myself to get frustrated and angry because I was trying to convince someone of something that they didn't want to be convinced of and/or weren't ready to listen to? (Or maybe you were just straight up wrong and trying to force a mistaken belief onto another... but let's put that aside for now).

For example, hopefully by now in this book you recognize that I have some wisdom that many don't. That I have knowledge that can help people and that I use that knowledge to help people heal all the time. But even I recognize that it is not my duty to heal people who aren't ready to be healed, who don't want my help, or who don't resonate with my messages. It is NOT my responsibility to convince anyone of the things I am sharing with you in this book. I don't shove this stuff down the throats of every person I meet. It is only my responsibility to share this wisdom with those who show me that they want it. You showed me that you wanted it by buying this book, but I'm not going to force anyone who doesn't want to read it, to read it, including my closest family and friends. No-one who does not want this wisdom owes me the obligation of reading it.

> The mantra I use for myself about this is; "share your wisdom with those who seek it, and for everyone else just shine your light."

Especially when I started going through my awakening and started recognizing and acknowledging higher perspective truths about the world and the universe (some spiritual concepts, some about society, many about emotions and psychology, etc.), I was still very unsure of myself. A lot was happening and a lot was changing for me, and even though there was a big part of me that was beginning to see and believe some new things, there was also a HUGE part of me that just wondered if I was going crazy, and I wasn't truly firm in my new beliefs and perspectives yet.

From within that energy, I was trying to tell people all around me about these new ideas I was becoming accustomed to, trying to shove it down their throats because I was finally starting to see these things for myself and because - unsure as I was about these things - I believed that they were of vital importance for all humanity. I THOUGHT that I was sharing this stuff with others from an altruistic "I'm trying to help you" point of view, but I realize now that I was really just seeking validation and approval, and - unfortunately - I was seeking it from people who weren't going to be capable of understanding me anyway, ESPECIALLY when I was coming at it from that energy.

When you try to explain new concepts to people and you are coming from an energy of "please believe me because I need someone to tell me that I'm not crazy", THAT is exactly when you start to sound crazy. You're basically pleading with people to believe something that even you - in that moment - are not fully comfortable believing. I was trying to explain these things to people because - deep down - I was desperately hoping that they were going to reassure me and validate these new beliefs that I was still struggling to accept. I convinced myself that it was altruism, when really it was insecurity and fear about what I was going through.

Eventually, when I finally learned my lessons and did some healing and became more able to accept the truths of my revelations even when met with resistance from people who couldn't resonate with them, THAT is when more people started listening to me - because I was able to approach the conversations and the topic from a much more 'matter-of-fact' energy. I was simply sharing what I knew and/or believed in. If they wanted to listen or believe me, that was cool, and if they didn't, then that was cool too! That took the pressure and the tension out of the conversation in a way that allowed people to relax and to consider my words for long enough to decide what they actually thought about it.

Once my energy of insecurity changed and I was no longer subconsciously pleading for their approval, the whole conversation changed and I was able to influence more people. When I was more at peace with myself and no longer needed validation, that's when I was able to start having a real impact.

More importantly, though, the more that I came to truly know, accept and believe my own truth without the need for validation, the less I found the need to try to explain it to people who weren't interested, and that's when I realized that - until that very moment - I had just been seeking approval because I hadn't yet developed enough self-love and enough confidence in my own beliefs to truly stand firmly in them. I wasn't explaining this stuff to people out of altruism before, I was doing it from pain, fear, and insecurity and I merely deluded myself into thinking that it was about saving others.

Start recognizing all the times that you find yourself trying to explain or justify your thoughts, actions, or beliefs to other people, and ask yourself why you are bothering to engage in an exchange like that. Do you truly believe that it is coming from a place of love, comfort, and peace inside of you, or is it coming from a place of insecurity? I think you'll find that the vast majority of the time (in fact, all of the time), when you are trying to convince someone who hasn't actively sought out your advice about something you believe in, that it's just coming from insecurity, and that everyone will be better off - particularly you - if you learn to just back off and let people go on their own journeys. Share your wisdom with those who seek it, and the rest of the time you should just choose self-love over the conflict and frustration that will undoubtedly be created by trying to force your beliefs - or even your divine wisdom - onto other people.

Do you want to actively cultivate this kind of argument and continue to attract frustration into your life, or do you want to maintain your own sense of inner peace so that you can progress in your life and healing journey and just learn to feel better on a daily basis? Do you want to justify your pain, or escape it? It's really a simple question. Even for those of you who believe - as I do - that you have a legitimate purpose on this Earth to help people heal, your moral obligation is not about pushing it onto people who haven't asked for it. Your 'divine mission' is not an excuse to preach your beliefs to everyone you meet. Your divine mission will play itself out naturally, and you'll help the people that you are meant to help because they will find you, not the other way around.

Now... none of this means that you shouldn't disagree with others or get into polite debates for the mutually beneficial growth of all the people involved. This doesn't mean 'just put yourself in an echo chamber and only ever talk to people who agree with everything you already believe and make you feel good about yourself no matter what'. That's not helpful and you will never grow, evolve, or heal if you simply push away anyone who doesn't think exactly what you think or who strokes your ego no matter what you say. That's not your goal. It's really just a matter of 'what energy and emotion am I bringing into a conversation', 'what energy and emotion is this other person bringing to the conversation' and 'is this conversation going to be mutually beneficial for us both at the intellectual and emotional levels, or is this just a battle of egos that is going to lead us nowhere?'

Whenever you can recognize that the conversation isn't going to be helpful or that you or the other person are actually just responding reflexively to uncomfortable emotions being triggered, you'll be faced with the real challenge of this section; do you have the strength, skill, and wisdom to politely walk away from a situation that is charged with unhelpful and negative emotional energy, or is your ego going to get the best of you and push you to keep arguing because you desperately need to be right or to receive their validation and approval?

This is when you need to shift to Mind Hack #3; take responsibility for yourself and your emotions, and recognize that for the sake of your own inner peace it will simply be more productive to walk away. Overall, the point of this section is to point out that what you think you are doing out of a sense of altruism is actually a triggered defense mechanism, and you need to turn your attention inwards to the things that you are saying and doing out of fear. The only reason you are trying to convince this person of something is because you are afraid - either - of what you think you believe but are unsure of, or of being looked down on by someone who doesn't believe and support the same idea.

Confronting that ego and that uncomfortable emotion inside of you that is trying to force you to argue will be very revealing for you. It will make you see more directly how this was never about being right or wrong. It was never about the thing you were actually arguing about. It was just about your own unstable sense of self-worth that you were trying to soothe by winning an argument or converting someone to your side. It was uncomfortable for you to be unsure of yourself, and you thought that it would soothe your pain to have this other person agree with you. It was never about ethics and a moral responsibility, it was never about altruism, it was never about educating others... it was about you not loving yourself enough to maintain the full truth of who you are when confronted with the contradicting opinions of another person and a need for others around you to agree with you, so that you could feel more self-assured in your own beliefs.

If you were fully self-assured of yourself in the first place, you wouldn't feel the need to push your beliefs onto others, and you would understand and accept that everyone needs to go on their own journeys and that you can only help those who want your help.

So, stop trying to explain yourself to others when they do not seem willing to hear you out, because you doing so is NOT the altruistic and helpful act you think it is... it is a cry for help and for validation from a part of you that is still suffering from past trauma and that is lacking the strength to stand in your own convictions when faced with resistance. Stop trying to convince the other person that you are right, and instead turn your attention to the uncomfortable emotions that are coming up inside of you that are pushing you to continue this useless argument and giving you the need to make them know you are right.

If you truly love yourself enough, then you won't feel the need to make them know you are right and you won't want to engage in the frustrating energy involved in a conversation with two people who aren't ready, willing, or able to truly hear each other.

When you master this skill, all of your conversations will remain more calm, pleasant, and mutually beneficial, and you will more skillfully, compassionately, and lovingly walk away or put an end to any conversation that isn't going to be helpful or enjoyable for anyone. You will also be able to impact more people, because they will be more willing to listen in the right moments.

EXTRA NOTE

For those of you who are experiencing a spiritual awakening, as I did, there is an extra layer to this.

We are often trying to explain this new, spiritual stuff that we are recognizing about the universe to other people, when they are literally incapable of understanding it. That's not a judgment, by the way, it's merely a fact of how this whole 'awakening' thing works.

Think about it this way... until YOU started going through your awakening, nothing anybody said could have possibly convinced you of the stuff that you are recognizing now, right? For example, I now recognize beyond the shadow of a doubt that Astral Travel is a real phenomenon, that 'Remote Viewing' is something that happens every day, and that you can actually learn and practice these skills.

But, until I started going through my own awakening (which happened on its own - I could not possibly have 'chosen' to go through it intentionally), absolutely nothing you could have said to me would have convinced me that this was real. It took me – probably – three years from the first time I saw a video about this stuff until I was able to actually accept it as reality. Five years ago, I would have rolled my eyes at you and walked out the door convinced that you were a complete idiot if you tried to convince me that Astral Projection was real. NOTHING you could have said would have convinced me.

Everyone has their own timeline to waking up to this stuff and you can't force anything. You CANNOT logically argue to an unawakened person about your new awakened realizations. It's not possible, because these are things that must be seen (or rather, felt) in order to be believed.

There is actually a movie called 'The Men Who Stare at Goats', about the CIA program in the 80's where they trained psychic spies. I watched the movie about ten years ago and it was absolutely hilarious. The characters were insane. The techniques they were trying were bonkers and the whole thing was a joke. A super enjoyable movie... and a joke. It was satire. No doubt.

I watched the movie again a few months ago... and it was basically a documentary to me. Still funny and satirical... but real. I saw the whole thing from a completely different perspective, simply because I was ready to. It happened naturally and on its own. It would have been impossible for me to see things that way back when I watched it the first time and I would have completely written off anyone who tried to tell me that it was real.

Interestingly, the movie actually begins with the disclaimer: "More of this is true than you would believe". When I saw that disclaimer on my second viewing, I realized that it was 100% accurate.

That's what makes this an 'awakening'. An evolution of our consciousness to be able to perceive things that were right in front of us this whole time, but that we simply did not have the cognitive or emotional capacity to observe and understand before. It's like trying to explain to a blind person what 'red' is, or trying to program a computer to feel love. There are no words that can possibly be strung together to explain concepts such as 'love' or 'red' to someone who does not yet have the faculties to perceive them.

There is no point in trying to explain this stuff to people who can't yet see it for themselves. In fact, doing so often pushes them further away from the truth when you are sharing it with them because - basically inevitably, based on everything I said above - you will be coming at the conversation from a place of insecurity and validation-seeking, rather than the true self-aware passion that might indeed be helpful to the other person.

> **You must be 100% in control of your own beliefs and your own emotions before you can truly and effectively guide others to raising their own consciousness and waking up for themselves.**

There is another reason why trying to explain this stuff to the unawakened can actually push them further away from the truth, which I like to call the "Agent Smith Effect". For those of you unaware, this is a reference to the 'Agents' in the *Matrix* movies – where all of humanity is enslaved into a false digital reality called "the Matrix". The agents are part of the programming of the Matrix, and they are connected to every single person that is still hard-wired to the system. The main job of the Agents is to prevent the 'Red Pills' (like Neo, Trinity, and Morpheus) from awakening others. When the Matrix is threatened by these Red Pills, Agent Smith can pop into anyone's body, take over, and fight against them.

This is what happens when you try to convince an unawakened person of higher dimensional truths. You're trying to make them see something that they are not ready to see, and - as Morpheus says - "You have to understand, most of these people are not ready to be unplugged. And many of them are so inert, so hopelessly dependent on the system that they will actually fight to protect it." When you try to 'wake someone up' before they are ready, the attachments they have to their current beliefs will trigger them into defending their old perspective and they will actively push against what you are trying to show them.

So... stop trying to explain this stuff to people and to get them to see what you yourself were unable to see not that long ago. The only thing that you can do to help people get there is to just BE the best, most compassionate, most loving version of yourself that you can be. By being that person, you have an impact and leave a mark on others that will help them relax, open up, and be willing to follow and listen to you if and when they are ready.

Just master yourself and your emotions, and BE LOVE. That's all you ever have to do. Everything else will fall into place naturally once you learn how to do that.

C - Stop Saying 'Anymore'.

(Note: this section will make the most sense to people on the roller coaster ride of spiritual awakening and - most specifically – to those on the twin flame journey, but the lesson absolutely applies to everyone. It just won't be as obvious to you why it's so important.)

There are certain words and phrases that program your mind in ways you don't fully realize, and one of those words is 'anymore'.

Often, we move in and out of stages of our lives - maybe we have feelings of love for someone one day and we don't the next, maybe we love one style of music one day and we don't the next, or maybe we feel a certain way one day and we don't the next. Life is always in flux and we are always changing. This is normal and to be expected. That is what life is all about.

66

We have a certain desire for stability, though. We don't like change most of the time, even when that change is something that's good for us, and we try to maintain some sense of control around our lives by constantly putting labels and descriptions onto what we are feeling at any given moment.

So, when we switch out of mode 'A' and into mode 'B' we often tell ourselves 'oh... I'm not feeling 'A' anymore'. Sometimes not feeling 'A' is a good thing and sometimes it's a bad thing... Sometimes you don't know which it is.

(Ok... The spiritual and somewhat awakened among us know that 'good' and 'bad' aren't real. We know that there is truly no 'good' or 'bad' and that it's all perception, but you know what I mean. We move from one state, feeling, or belief to another and we tend to think of one of them as 'good' and the other as 'bad', and when we shift into state 'B' we tend to say to ourselves, 'well, I guess I'm not in state 'A' anymore'.)

The point is that; when you put the word 'anymore' onto a shift that you just experienced, you are unintentionally making a determination that keeps you stuck and attached to one version of reality, which you then cling onto even more. You are constantly trying to make these definitive statements about your life to help you analyze where you're at, when really the truth of the matter is that things are just shifting all the time.

Maybe you had feelings of love for that person yesterday and you're not feeling that today. That's fine. But if you put the word 'anymore' there ("I don't have feelings for this person anymore"), then you are making a determination that part of you is going to want to stick to, at least at the subconscious level. You are telling your heart and brain that you have moved past that other state, and you're basically trying to convince yourself not to shift back into that state. You are making a statement that the other state (that other perspective and part of your life) is over and that you should never move back to it. So, tomorrow morning when you wake up and you're thinking about that person again and you DO feel something for them again, it's just going to create more conflict, frustration, and annoyance in you that you 'didn't have feelings for them anymore', and now you do again, and then you won't anymore, etc.

By using the word 'anymore', you are trying to force yourself in a particular direction, and if your heart chooses to go back and forth on this a bit (which it will sometimes do), you are just going to create more unease and frustration within yourself because you had spent all of this time telling yourself that you were 'so done' with that old feeling. You think that you are using the word 'anymore' to describe how you are feeling right now, but it is actually a word that is subconsciously programming yourself for how you think you should feel in the future. When you say 'anymore', you are telling yourself that you will not switch back into that state in the future, and this will cause more distress if your heart actually does switch back.

Why do you feel the need to determine at this very moment whether what you feel right now is going to last into the future? Why do you need to describe what you are experiencing right now as the be all and end all of what you are going to experience around this thought, idea, belief, or feeling? Wouldn't it be so much easier for you to replace the word 'anymore' with the phrase 'right now' so that your future can be more open-ended? This will help you stay out of fear, and to stay in a state of acceptance and surrender to whatever you are feeling in any moment.

"I don't feel those feelings for them right now".

"I don't feel my connection to the universe right now".

"I don't enjoy rap music right now."

Phrasing things like this keeps your experience open ended. You don't get attached to the emotional state that you're in right now and you are allowing things to flow in whatever direction they want to. If you wake up tomorrow and have feelings for that person again, OK. If you wake up tomorrow and don't feel a connection to them, that's ok too. You can't force how you're going to feel about anything or what's going to happen in the future, and if you keep saying 'anymore' when something changes, then you will be more committed and attached to a certain version of reality that will make it all the more painful and confusing when it changes again.

> Everything happens in waves. The only unchanging aspect of our reality is that there is always change.

Replace 'anymore' with 'right now' and you will always be freer to flow into whatever the future wants to reveal to you. Don't use words that commit yourself to a certain version of the future, because the future won't usually be what you thought it would and you will spend so much energy trying to justify the things that you once said when you were in another state.

Don't try to control things so much (even unconsciously). Trying to control things is really based in fear, and you don't want to cultivate fear inside of yourself anymore.

D - Stop Saying 'Don't Believe'.

This is a small one, but one I would like to add in anyway because I believe that it can have a positive effect for a lot of people as we start opening ourselves up to new concepts and as the world goes through some major paradigm shifts.

There are a lot of opposing opinions coming to light every day. A lot of new technologies, a lot of new understandings about the world and the universe and everything going on all around us, and it is getting harder and harder for a lot of people to agree on all sorts of things. This just creates more separation, more fear, more anger, etc. We need to do as much as possible to enter into an understanding between each other, or to merely maintain compassion and kindness for people who are not on the same page as us.

For that reason, I suggest that whenever you are confronted with an opinion or piece of information that doesn't immediately sit well or resonate with you, instead of using the phrase 'I don't believe that', instead say 'I don't understand'. Phrasing things in this way will allow you to keep an open conversation with people who don't believe what you do and vice versa, and it will allow everyone to continue expressing themselves more freely until we can come to an understanding between each other.

You will find that when you take the time to understand why others believe something that you do not, you will almost always find some kind of common ground. In general, it's really a matter of language and other illusory superficial things that are getting in the way of you uniting as people. At the end of the day, we all believe in the same things - love, kindness, living in peace, etc. That's what everyone wants at the end of the day. It is only because of our pain and millennia of programming that we have put all these labels and boundaries on all the concepts that we believe separate us as people. It is the words, symbols and language that separate us, not our core truths.

As I was saying earlier, you cannot possibly find any string of words to truly describe what 'red' or 'love' are. The same goes for things like 'faith', 'god', 'morality', 'justice', 'ethics'... these are the grand concepts that we all carry with us somewhere inside of us, but because we all tried to put strict definitions and codes onto those grand concepts, they became something that we can argue and fight over.

At the end of the day, all religions are pointing to the same truths - that we are all one, that we are all a part of god, that love is the answer, etc. Even science and religion are ultimately pointing at the same truth (ex: the Big Bang... we all came from one singularity). We're all looking towards the same truth. We are all just looking at it through different lenses, and if we can come to realize that our differences are a superficial matter of understanding, not core human beliefs, then we can come to understand each other that much more quickly.

Begin to recognize that - at our cores - we are all one and we are all aimed in the same direction. Any disagreements about these grand concepts are coming either from misunderstandings or from pain. Our differences are superficial, but our similarities go right to the core. When you can let go of judgment and choose to try and understand why someone believes something that contradicts what you believe, you will always find common ground. You just need to put down your shields and swords first. When we stop fighting each other because we are so insecure about our own beliefs, we will realize that there was nothing to fight over in the first place.

So, when someone presents a belief or thought that contradicts something you have been basing your life around, choose to say "I don't understand you" instead of "I don't believe that". This will open up the doors for mutual growth and understanding.

E - Stop Swearing

This one might be a little more 'controversial' or perhaps just less agreed on - or some of you might just not like it or want to stop - so... take it or leave it.

Many spiritual or supposedly unconditionally loving people like to support the idea that you can be spiritual and still tell people to 'fuck off'. Some people like to use 'fuck' or other swears even as a mantra of meditation to help them release frustration in a moment. I'm sorry to say, but I believe this is a mistake. I believe that the emotion attached to these words is actually a negative and self-harming one that you do NOT want to be actively programming into yourself.

Yes... Some studies have shown that swearing can help us withstand pain or get a sense of relief in the moment. I'm not denying that... I'm suggesting that - as usual - there is simply a misunderstanding of how this works.

I think that saying 'fuck' in a moment of frustration DOES in fact provide an instantaneous sense of relief like people think, but it does so in the same way that punching the person who annoyed you in the face might. It is a way of bypassing the uncomfortable emotions that you are feeling in a moment and projecting your anger outwards. It is actively allowing yourself to get angry for a moment, which feels good when there is an uncomfortable emotion trying to work its way through you that you don't want to feel, because swearing brings up the same negative frequency inside of you as the frequency of frustration or anger that's trying to move through you in that moment.

There is a sense of relief because you are bringing yourself into alignment with the negative emotion, by reinforcing that negative emotion with your conscious thoughts. Relief happens because you are attuning yourself to the pain of the situation, intentionally diving deeper into it. It's not actually helpful, but it does feel good. It feels better than allowing an uncomfortable emotion to freely run through you in a way that will allow it to get processed and released. Saying "fuck" helps you project your uncomfortable feeling outwards. It helps you turn your emotional discomfort into a projectile of anger, fear or judgment.

There is an emotion of anger, resentment, judgment, or anything else that is trying to work its way through you in that moment, and by swearing you basically acclimate yourself to that emotion. You align yourself with it.

Instead of allowing the uncomfortable emotion to work through you so that it can be released, you program yourself to shift even more INTO that negative emotion. That feels good in the moment because it alleviates the misalignment within yourself (since both your head and your heart are now in 'anger', there is less disagreement inside of you and therefore less discord), but the

72

pleasurable feeling is actually because you just allowed yourself to slip even more into a negative emotion that was actually trying to get released. You swear to help align yourself with the negative emotion that is coming up, and that's not a good thing.

Think of it this way; what actually causes suffering in you is never the situation nor is it your thoughts and words. Suffering comes from the inner battle inside of you. One part of you that is trying to live in love and another part of you that is experiencing pain. These two conflicting energies living together in the same space cause the deepest layers of our suffering. It is the battle between these energies that does it. In order to relieve this suffering, we need to end the inner conflict, and this can be done in one of two ways; you can transmute the pain that you are feeling into love inside of you by feeling it, healing it and releasing it, or you can allow yourself to shift into negativity, anger, and frustration. Either option will give you a sense of instantaneous relief, but only one of them is actually having a positive impact on your life.

Basically, the emotional frequency of 'fuck' is certainly not love. That's all there is to it. The frequency of "shit", "bitch", etc. is not love. Saying these words or hearing them doesn't feel like love. Compare the emotion you feel when these words come up to a feeling of true inner peace and compassion that you might rather be focusing on in that moment, and I believe you'll see things the same way.

If not... then swear away, mother-fucker!

But... let me ask you; how did that last sentence FEEL to you? Did it feel as nice as the rest of this book, or did it feel at least a little more uncomfortable to read? Did me using that phrase help open up your heart or did it create more tension in your body?

Think about it. I believe you'll find that swearing is just cultivating more negative emotions inside of you, and you'll start realizing that you are harming yourself by allowing these words to flow through you all the time.

GOT A MINUTE?

Hey there!

Quick interruption. Are you enjoying this book? Are you finding it helpful? Do you believe that it can help others and that the ideas in this book are worth sharing?

Do you believe that the world would be a better place if more people understood the things that you are learning here and if more people dove into this healing?

If so, please take a minute right now and go leave a review for this book on Amazon or on GoodReads. This will go a long way to helping others know that there is valuable information here.

Then, **please** consider making a post about this book on social media.

Thank you so much for taking the time! It truly means a lot to me, and it will help spread these important lessons and push us collectively to a brighter world.

A digital copy of this book can be purchased at http://BenjyShererCoaching.com/mhbook. Physical copies and Kindle versions can be found on Amazon and some other online retailers. Audiobooks are also available.

Now, back to the book.

6

Put Your Feelings First

This one might seem a little vague at first, but it is the most important shift that you need to make and it is the one which all the Mind Hacks in this book - and the whole healing journey that you are on right now - revolve around. This is the ultimate goal of all the work that you are doing here, so it is important to spend a bit of time talking about this goal directly.

Our mission - through this awakening and healing process - is to learn how to get out of our heads and into our hearts. Your brain is an asshole. Your brain is outdated. Your heart truly knows what's up and can give you all the guidance that you'll need, if only you'll learn to listen and to put aside the fear-based thoughts of your old-school brain for long enough to hear what your heart is actually telling you. Basically, it's time for your brain to retire. Your brain can go play shuffleboard and bingo on the beach in Florida with its other retired friends. It has done its job... It fought in all the wars. It protected you when you needed to be protected, but you're safe now, and it's time to start living like it.

It's time to start putting your *Feelings First* and listening to your heart - above and beyond what your head is telling you. Your head is still living like you're at war, and it's just not helpful or pleasant.

So... what do I mean by 'put your feelings first'?

There are four main ideas here:

A - Recognize that emotions actually came first.

This first lesson is something we've already touched on a bit in this book, but it certainly bears repeating and clarification as much as possible; Your brain has been deluding itself into thinking it has been in charge. You have actually been a slave to your emotions in more ways than you've ever stopped to realize, and all of your decisions that you thought were based on logic were actually made first from emotions, and then justified with logic after-the-fact.

If our goal is emotional mastery, then we need to learn to turn our attention to our emotions directly, more and more quickly, all the time in our day-to-day lives. How can we get in control of our emotional reactions if we keep ignoring the role that emotions are playing in guiding our decisions? We need to practice interrupting the old thought patterns that are focused on solving problems in the outside world and that thereby allow us to ignore what's going on inside of ourselves.

We have been trained throughout our lives to push our feelings aside in order to survive in the world and to be a productive member of society. We have forced ourselves to separate emotions from the other areas of our lives. So, it's no wonder that we can't hear what our hearts are trying to tell us and that we don't even recognize that they've been guiding us this whole time.

So, in order to raise our consciousness, to take control of our emotions, and to make true progress with our inner healing, we need to start putting more active intention on recognizing the emotional root of our behavior. We need to recognize that emotions actually hit us instantaneously whereas a thought takes some time. It takes at least a second or two to think the phrase "well, that was rude", but it only takes an instant to feel offended by someone's rude behavior. The emotion hit first and instantaneously. The thought was a reaction to - and byproduct of - that emotion.

Until we can recognize that the emotion came first, we will continue to justify the emotion rather than observe and heal it.

I actually just received this message from a client today that will help express this point:

"I just noticed all my thoughts this morning after I did my inner child meditation. Thoughts that had the theme of self-doubt and I was like "oh yeah, that's the feeling I need to feel and process". So, I felt it and then I felt better and I stopped having self-doubt thoughts! Then it dawned on me that this is what you have been talking about the whole time. My self-doubt thoughts were not just coming from the neural pathways I've created by thinking the thoughts my whole life, they were coming from an unprocessed emotion."

This client was finally able to see how her thoughts of self-doubt were actually symptoms of an unprocessed emotion and - because she recognized this - she was able to confront, heal, and release the emotion directly and not get triggered by it, so that she could progress on her healing journey. She was able to end the thoughts of self-doubt by recognizing the raw emotional root of the problem. She used to think that her self-doubt issues were all based in 'rational' issues about her past traumas and thoughts. Now she realized that it was actually all emotional. The more that she can recognize this about all her self-harming thoughts and behavior, the more invulnerable to negativity she will become and the better her life will get.

Granted, she is just about finishing my course as I write this, so it took about 7 weeks of us working together to get her to this point, but this is exactly where you are trying to get to. Still, only 7 weeks to undo a lifetime's worth of self-doubt? Not bad!

> If you want to achieve the same kind of freedom from your self-doubt, guilt, shame, anxiety, or more then you should check out my 8-week course on Self-Love and Shadow Work, here: http://BenjyShererCoaching.com/ffcourse

B - Prioritize your emotional wellness.

Secondly, you need to start recognizing that your emotional health and your emotional state are the most important things for you to care for at any given moment. Learning how to stay in a state of self-love and compassion is the most important work you will ever do in this lifetime. Seriously.

It's just like the protocol on airplanes where, when the oxygen masks come down, you need to put on your own mask before helping others because - until you are safe and taken care of - you can't be responsible for others.

It works exactly the same way with your emotions. Until you are stable within yourself, you have nothing solid to offer to others. Self-love and self-care MUST come first if you want to be of benefit to the world. The more that you drain yourself in the name of 'helping others' without taking care of yourself first, the less that you will have to offer to others, and no-one wins. The more that you martyr yourself, the less energy you will have to offer the world. If you want to give to the world everything that you possibly can, then you need to attend to yourself first.

> Self-love is not selfish. It is ABSOLUTELY NECESSARY.

Equally as importantly, though, by mastering your own emotions you will learn how to be more compassionate, patient, kind, caring, unconditionally loving, supportive, etc. By prioritizing your emotions, you will develop the very skills that the world most sorely needs right now. You don't need to do anything special to help change the world. You certainly don't need to write books or teach shadow work like I do. You just need to learn how to stop playing the 'anger and fear' game that society has been playing for a long time, and how to love yourself enough to not get triggered when other people put their own pain and fear onto you.

Humans have been playing the 'anger game' for a long time. People were not realizing how much pain they were carrying inside of them, because they didn't understand things like 'trauma' and how it affected them psychologically. They were not realizing how they were perpetuating their own suffering by projecting their pain onto the outside world. Think about it... you're basically just learning a lot of that stuff right now, in this very book. 100 years ago and more people certainly didn't realize it. No-one understood the cyclical nature of pain and trauma.

So, everyone was walking around with all of their insecurities hanging out, with their triggers and traumas and defense mechanisms on display and in control. When one person got triggered, they would get defensive and angry and act in a defensive and angry way that then made the first person who triggered them get angrier and react in anger, causing the second person to get triggered more, and around and around they went. Anger kept fueling anger all because no-one realized that they were actually just in pain, that this other person was also just in pain, and that everyone was just trying to avoid feeling their pain. It was a useless game of letting anger grow and grow inside of and between themselves.

Do you know what causes feedback in a speaker? That loud and awful blaring noise that we've all heard at some point when some drunk person picks up a microphone at a wedding or when a sound check at a concert isn't going well?

Here's what's happening in that moment: the sound that is going into the microphone comes out of the speaker. From there, that sound goes back into the microphone, which then comes back out of the speaker, and back into the microphone, then back out of the speaker, etc. This happens 10,000 times in a second, and every time it happens the sound wave amplifies itself and gets bigger and bigger because it's the same frequency happening over and over. It stacks itself larger and larger. When one frequency gets applied to an equivalent frequency - they amplify each other, growing stronger and stronger with every instance of repetition.

This is exactly what has been happening with anger, fear, judgment, defensiveness, etc. Someone gives you anger, and that triggers anger inside of you which makes you get angry at the other person, which triggers anger inside of them and makes them get angry at you, which triggers anger inside of you, etc. This keeps on happening over and over until at least one person in this dynamic notices it and is able to stop playing that 'anger game'.

We need as many people as possible to start understanding that their anger and insecurities are their own, so that when someone gives them anger, they can remain calm and give the other person patience and compassion instead of more anger. By doing this, we stop adding more and more anger to the world and we allow the other people the space to maybe relax for a minute and (subconsciously) go, 'hmm... I don't have to be defensive with this person. I can let my guard down and be open'. Slowly, we will all start letting go of our defensiveness.

It only takes one person to be ready to do this in order to change the entire dynamic of a relationship or conversation. When one person stops playing the anger game, that game ends and both parties need to figure out how to play a new game together, or they need to stop playing any game between themselves at all. By prioritizing your emotional wellness, you become the person that you are meant to be and you allow others the space to determine whether they want to keep playing their old game or to grow and evolve alongside you.

Most people have never had the opportunity to even consider not playing the anger game anymore, because NO-ONE in their lives has ever been able to give them compassion and understanding in the face of the pain that they are masking through their bad behavior. Never before have they been given the safe space and dynamics to let go of their defense mechanisms for a moment and to truly feel and express their emotions freely. In every other circumstance and relationship in their lives they had to be on guard and defensive, and you - if you master yourself - might be the very first person to show them that they are safe.

When you stop playing the anger game, you give others the opportunity to stop playing it as well. If they agree to stop playing it, you both get to change the dynamics of your relationship together. If they don't, then as a matter of self-love you will learn to walk away - without judgment or anger about it. This becomes possible when you start prioritizing the emotions that you feel in a moment (and prioritizing feelings of love) rather than defending your ego and prioritizing your conscious thoughts, beliefs, actions, and decisions.

Prioritizing your emotional wellness also means just putting this healing journey that you are on at the top of your list. There is nothing more important than this healing, so make sure that this is where your energy is going, because - as you achieve emotional mastery - all of the other areas of your life are going to start falling into place much more easily anyway.

When you are truly feeling unafraid and you are acting from unconditional self-love as your foundation, you will start making decisions, taking actions and choosing friendships and relationships that are going to make your life better. It will create an upwards spiral of growth and progress. When you're acting defensively because you prioritize your cognitive experience over your emotional one, on the other hand, you play into that 'fear and anger game' and it keeps you on a negative spiral.

> Put your attention onto your emotions first, because mastering your emotions will make everything else better.

And hey... even if it doesn't have the practical effects on your life towards the practical outcome that you want it to... you'll be feeling better about whatever is happening in your life because you've mastered your emotions! That's the beautiful paradox that sits at the center of this inner healing journey. Regardless of the external consequences, your life will be more pleasant because you chose this route and THEN your life can start actually getting better at the practical level.

C - Solve the Emotion before the 'Problem'.

This is an extension of what we were just discussing, but basically, it's a reminder that - in any given moment and whatever the world throws at you - the only REAL problem that you have is not what just happened in the external world, but rather how you feel about it. If you master your emotions first and learn to truly feel at peace with whatever happens to you in this world, then there can't really be any true problems... can there? If you can feel good about whatever is happening, then that's all that matters and there is no problem.

Obviously, we are all human and none of us are trying to literally be the Buddha, so it's ok that there are limits to how far you are willing to take this concept, but the more that you can understand the ultimate universal truth behind it, the easier life will be. It is extremely possible to be broke and alone, and to not suffer at all as a result of that at the emotional level. Without attachment, without expectation... there is no real problem. Whereas it's also possible to be rich and have everything you could ever want and to be miserable about all of it. The problem isn't whether or not you have money or a partner or any of that stuff, the only problem is in how you feel about it, and in the attachment and desires you have to specific outcomes.

You want to start practicing and realizing this so that you can more quickly turn your attention to the REAL problem in any situation, which is how you feel about whatever is happening. Let's fix your internal reaction so that there is no actual problem anymore. Let's overcome the ONLY 'real' problem that is happening in the moment. Once you are in that space emotionally where you are calm and at peace with whatever you are experiencing, THEN you can turn your attention to what happened in the outside world, and - as a result of this calm and centered reaction - you will always end up with better outcomes.

When you focus on the external problem first, you react defensively, aggressively, judgmentally, etc. and this will lead you to more and more problems on a downwards spiral caused by the triggering of unresolved emotions. When you focus on the internal problem first, on the other hand, you will feel better that much more quickly and - as a result of feeling better - you will take better actions that lead to better outcomes. This is the upwards spiral you want to be on.

Emotions must come first!

D - Follow your emotions.

Lastly, prioritizing your emotions means that you should place what your heart is telling you at the top of the list when it comes to making decisions. Your heart knows what's best, even when your head doesn't understand.

This is extremely difficult for most of us because we have been living in our heads our whole lives and have actively (but subconsciously) built a wall up around our hearts; but when you can learn to truly trust your heart and your intuition, your life becomes SO easy. It's kind of crazy how simple life can be when you master the art of following and trusting your heart. You don't need to rationalize everything. You don't need to understand everything or plan out every possible outcome to every possible scenario. You get to relax into the moment knowing that - at any given moment - your heart is going to guide you in the right direction.

This is how you let go of stress and worry, which are all about imagined versions of the future that don't exist. There are immensely positive versions of the future that are just as likely as the negative ones that you are imagining, but your brain doesn't occupy its energy with 'what if everything goes really, really well for me?'. Nope. Your brain's favorite game to play is "what should I worry about today?"

This is how your brain attempts to stay in control. It analyzes all the ways that you got hurt in the past and calculates all the possible ways that this could happen again in the future to help you avoid experiencing that pain again. The only reason it does this is because it knows that the last time something like that event happened, there was emotional pain that it didn't know how to deal with and because it still feels wary of confronting that same pain. Your brain is desperately trying to avoid confronting the thing that it didn't want to confront the first time around.

Your brain is just a coward that's still too scared to deal with the uncomfortable emotions that it stuffed away in the first place. It's just a band-aid that your brain is scared to rip-off, and so the wound is getting infected underneath this rotten, old band-aid. It's afraid to feel the momentary pain of confronting your emotions head on. You can't hear what your heart is telling you through love, because you are so desperately trying to avoid hearing what it's telling you through pain.

Your brain is telling you that a certain action will lead to emotional distress that it doesn't know how to deal with, and so you should go in the other direction. Prudent while that might be, it is certainly no way to live life. It is all based in fear. So, you need to start allowing your heart to guide you, even when it is going to mean confronting some unpleasant and uncomfortable emotions, because doing so is the only way to start healing and to realign yourself with the direction you're meant to be moving in.

Now, there are perhaps some mixed messages here. On the one hand I'm saying that you need to notice how your emotions are at the root of your actions and take steps to change that, and on the other hand I'm saying that you need to learn to follow your emotions. I get that this might be confusing, but there is actually no contradiction here at all.

To explain it simply, you need to learn how to notice and change your actions that are based in anger, fear, doubt, shame, etc. While at the same time learning how to notice and follow emotions like joy, love, passion, etc. In order to learn how to follow the positive emotions, you are first going to need to learn how to notice, heal, confront, and release the negative ones. You are trying to learn to allow love to guide you, and in order to do that you will first need to notice and release all the ways that fear has been holding you back. You WANT your emotions to guide you, you just want different emotions to guide you than the ones that have been in charge so far, and you want to become more aware of all of the ways that your emotions have been guiding you, so that you can actively choose to follow the positive ones, instead of passively allowing yourself to keep subconsciously being manipulated by the negative ones.

Avoiding a situation because you are afraid of the emotional distress that comes along with it is very different from avoiding a situation because you love yourself too much to bother with it. In each case the action is the same, but the motivating emotion is different. You are trying to learn how to follow your emotions in the direction of love.

The 4 words to transform your life.

To help you put this whole 'put your emotions first' thing into practice, your mind hack for this section is a simple four word phrase. Your goal is to remind yourself to repeat these words as often as possible throughout your day.

The phrase is: "How do I feel?"

Simple... no?

But really, until this very moment in your life, how often have you paused in your day-to-day life to check in with what is going on inside? How much of your energy and focus has been going to tackling problems in the outside world vs. attending to the problems of your inner world? We all have a habit of trying to solve how we feel by fixing the thing that we think caused that feeling, but when you can recognize and remember that the emotion came first and that this is all actually coming from unresolved pain still trapped inside of you, you can start creating real change and real solutions that will provide lasting benefits.

By continually repeating the words "how do I feel?" and doing quick inner check-ins, you will build the conscious connection with your body and your feelings that will keep you present, centered, and focused on creating a truly positive upwards spiral in your life. You will practice this connection and build the muscles so that you can start living from a heart-centered space, in more alignment with who you are.

When you ask yourself this question, check in with yourself. Notice your:

- Breathing
- Posture
- Heart rate
- Muscle tension
- Emotions

Go through each of these things and see where you're at. If appropriate and if you can, try to adjust. If you notice - for example - that you are breathing heavily or fast, calm your breath for a moment and come back to center. If you are hunched over, straighten up. If you notice yourself holding on to a lot of tension in your muscles and flexing or tensing up in any way, focus on relaxing and releasing it for a moment, etc.

If you do this repeatedly you will become more in tune with yourself as a whole, more connected to the present moment, and less able to be triggered or thrown off by the outside world.

Over and over and over throughout your day you want to ask yourself "how do I feel?", and perform this check: Breathing, posture, heart rate, muscles, emotions. The ultimate goal is to live in a state where you are always connected with how you feel, so that you can be more aware of how your feelings are guiding your actions.

I recommend connecting this practice with Mind Hack #1 from this book, "Programming Subroutines". Program this question and check in as a subroutine into your brain, reminding yourself to ask it as often as possible. Find something you do very often throughout the day, and choose to program this subroutine or use the dot on your hand or a piece of jewelry. The benefits you will see will astound you as you begin to connect much more quickly to what is happening inside of yourself in any situation.

These inner emotional/energetic sensations tell you MUCH more quickly than your thoughts when something is going wrong (or going well). Connecting to your body will improve your life in ways you can't yet imagine.

***

PS - The end of a chapter called "Put Your Feelings First" seems like an appropriate time to remind you of the partner book to this one, *'Feelings First Shadow Work: A Simple Approach to Self Love and Emotional Mastery'*. If you are enjoying this book of Mind Hacks, you will absolutely love the other book as well, and pairing the two together is ultimately more powerful than either of them on their own.

> You can pick up a physical copy on Amazon or other online retailers, or grab the eBook or get more info at http://BenjyShererCoaching.com/ffbook.

7

Your Physical Reality

There is a constant co-creation happening between your inner world and your outer world. Your environment, surroundings, and physical embodiment impact your thoughts and behavior which in turn play a role in determining what your environment, surroundings, and embodiment will be, and around and around we go. Part of what an 'awakening' is about is finally raising your consciousness far enough out of your limited viewpoint to recognize the co-creation cycles and your role in manifesting your life circumstances, so that you may start taking better control of your life.

In fact, hopefully, by now you are realizing that the majority of what we are talking about overall in this book is self-perpetuating cycles that you simply never realized were happening, and how much easier it can be than you think to start changing those cycles - if you simply put your attention onto them for a moment.

By recognizing this co-creation pattern between your inner world and your outer world and by taking control of it, you become the conscious creator of your own life and things start improving in natural and self-perpetuating ways.

As you continue to work on your inner self, you need to make sure that your physical reality is supporting this journey that you're going on instead of dragging you down. Right now, your physical reality is a reflection and representation of all the decisions you've made in your life so far. It is a mirror image to the pre-healed version of you. So, as you raise the frequency of your inner world, you need to make sure that your physical reality is following suit.

You need to make sure that there is a positive feedback loop happening between your inner world and your outer world, and there are things that you can do to adjust your physical reality to help accelerate your emotional healing.

Here are two of my favorites that we touch on in my Emotional Mastery Course.

Letting Go of the Past

This is partly a Mind Hack, and partly a reversal of a subconscious mind hack that you didn't realize you were already performing to your own detriment. Holding on to keepsakes and lovingly reminiscing about our past is fine, but most of us are holding on to too much and are preventing ourselves from moving forward in our lives by keeping certain objects around. There's a very fine line between a healthy nostalgia and toxic over-attachment.

By NOT clearing out certain old things from your environment, you are subconsciously programming yourself to stay stuck. It is keeping you tied to a version of yourself and of reality that no longer resonates with where you are, and it keeps you from growing and evolving in a healthy way. Keeping these objects around is subconsciously programing your identity and keeping you stuck in an old version of who you once were - both energetically and consciously. It is preventing you from letting go of the past and evolving as a person.

There are three main reasons that you would hold onto things from the past that are no longer useful to you, and none of them are good.

The first potential reason is that there is unresolved trauma around that time period in your life. You sometimes hold onto objects because you are emotionally connected to them in a negative way, or to the era of your life associated with those objects.

You hold onto them because trying to get rid of them would force you to confront emotions that you don't feel ready to deal with. This is very common when dealing with the death of a loved one. If you don't deal with the emotions of grief when they are fresh, they stick around, embed themselves deeply and covertly into your identity and personality, and it becomes harder to bring them up again to release them, but they are always there in the background, controlling your life in ways that you don't realize.

It is very important to let go of objects like these, but it's also important to do it in the right way. If you're holding onto things from a painful period in your past like this (or a beautiful period that ended in pain), my suggestion is not to simply rush to throw them away. Don't necessarily leap out of your chair right now, throw them in a trash bag, and toss them out the window before you have a moment to think. These objects are representations of buried pain. They are there to remind you of the pain that is holding you down and if you don't use this as an opportunity to deal with that pain, then - even though throwing them away is still progress - there are still a lot of trapped emotions surrounding this period of your life.

These objects represent an opportunity. They are tangible things that connect you to your past pain, and - as you should know by now - in order to heal from your past pain you need to connect to it, feel it, and allow it to be processed through you. This means that the act of going through and getting rid of these kinds of objects can help you heal from the trauma that you never resolved in the first place. If you just rush right now to throw these things out without stopping to take the time and make use of this opportunity to heal, then it will be harder for you to reconnect to these feelings and traumas in the future. Don't deprive yourself of this opportunity to heal because you're in a rush to move on. That would just be - once again - based in fear of feeling your emotions. Instead, you should relish and cherish the opportunity to deal with this pain in a safe environment.

I suggest going through the objects intentionally. Actively push yourself to focus on the feelings that they evoke inside of you and use this as an opportunity to release those emotions.

You can (for example) place all of the items from a time in your life in a room around you, and meditate or reflect on them. Actively allow yourself to go through all of the emotions that come up when focusing on them or remembering the time in your life from which they came. Remember... you are safe now. That time of your life is over and your emotions can't hurt you. There is nothing to fear. If you push away your emotions you will continue to suffer, but if you just allow them to run through you without fear and resistance right now, then not only will you be healthier, happier, and stronger because of it, but it will actually feel good!

Allowing old emotions to run through you - even the painful ones - without resistance is incredibly freeing, and like I said, you have nothing to fear. So... dive into it. Let it happen. Have the best cry of your life, let go of some old pain, and fill that space up with love and gratitude instead. It's beautiful. The more that you learn not to fear or resist those emotions, the more you'll learn that releasing them actually does just feel good. It's only resistance that causes the pain.

The second reason you might hold onto an object is because you are just afraid to move on with your life. Maybe you have a lot of sports trophies from high school that you're holding on to because those were your glory days. Especially if you're no longer an athlete, then you're holding on to these things because they represent a version of you that you are still clinging on to and - whether or not you realize it - allowing your identity to remain rooted in the past -

when that past version of you no longer reflects who you are - prevents you from growing.

The healthiest thing to do is to let go of all the things that are keeping you rooted in an outdated version of your identity that is no longer representative of who you can or should be.

I'm not exactly saying that you shouldn't have mementos, and photos, and keepsakes from your life. And yet... I kind of am. I'm pointing out that the ULTIMATELY FREE, buddha level versions of ourselves really WOULD get rid of all things that are no longer representative of us and no longer helpful – and that we would be emotionally and spiritually better off if we did so. At least, that version of ourselves wouldn't be attached to those objects and to the old versions of ourselves in the same way. We don't necessarily need to get rid of things if we genuinely hold nothing but love for ourselves and the past, but usually - as I've been saying - we are holding on to – at least some of - these things not from love, but rather from fear of evolving, growing, and letting go of the past.

So, it's not actually the objects that you need to let go of. You don't necessarily need to get rid of everything from the past. It's the fear of letting go and the attachment to them that you need to overcome. Achieving this will likely require that you get rid of SOME of the things that you really don't need (to practice and truly learn to accept letting go of things), but you don't need to get rid of everything. You just need to understand your attachments and fears.

Not all genuinely devoted Buddhists - for example - subscribe to the idea that you need to be without possessions or that you need to be poor. The idea is that you can freely own objects... so long as you are certain that those objects don't own you. If you can eliminate the fear, desire and attachment around the things that you consider to be 'yours', then you can freely hold on to them without causing yourself any problems. If you are afraid to let go of them, though... then you truly need to get rid of them.

I don't expect myself or anyone reading this book to want to go to extreme lengths of minimalism and detachment, but you should at least be mindful of what you're keeping around and why. Whether or not you choose to get rid of some old stuff, you at least need to make sure that you **would be** ok with letting them go. You need to release any attachment to the past that is too deep and holding you back. You need to confront the uncomfortable emotions that are associated with releasing these positive or negative periods from your past. If and when you have truly resolved these emotions, then getting rid of the objects or not becomes a genuine choice. Anything that you hold onto because it evokes a feeling of love or joy is perfectly acceptable and beneficial, but anything that you are holding onto because you are afraid to let go of the past, to accept the present, or to move confidently into the future is a problem.

Who you were 10 years ago is not who you are today, and that is a good thing. Don't try to be or to glorify who you were 10 years ago. Just focus on being the best version of whoever it is you are right now. Some people age gracefully, others hold on to the past. Clinging to an old version of yourself will only cause pain. Guaranteed.

The third reason you might hold onto something is because you are afraid that you might need it later and not have it. While perhaps prudent and practical, this kind of reasoning comes from a lack mentality. A belief in having 'not enough'. Especially if the thing that you're clinging on to has outlived its usefulness (at least in the moment), holding on to it stems from fear that you won't have what you need in the future, and any decisions that are made from fear simply reinforce fear inside of you and keep you on a negative spiral.

Every business guru in the world will tell you that the one thing that will keep you poor for certain more than anything else is a poverty mindset. Thinking like a poor man will ensure that you always remain a poor man (...or woman). If something is no longer useful or no longer getting used, trust that if you need something like it again in the future, you will get it.

Let it go. Move on.

To fully explain why this is the case - why you need to let go of things that you are holding onto as a result of a lack mentality - we will need to dive into the concept and theory behind 'law of attraction' and 'manifesting'. Fortunately, mind hack #10 is all about that stuff! We'll get there. For now, just recognize that holding on to something that is no longer useful because you're worried that you might need it in the future (especially when you have no specific reason to think that you will), is a decision that is based in fear and which will therefore breed more fear and more pain.

This will become incredibly obvious when you go to try to get rid of it right now. You'll notice the resistance in you about disposing of it and - hopefully, by now - you can recognize how that tense, resistance feeling around the decision that you call 'prudence' or 'practicality' is actually fear. Hopefully you can recognize the discomfort of that emotion and how the frequency of that feeling is quite the opposite of love, trust, and faith. If you trusted yourself and the universe enough, you'd let go of that which no longer serves you, knowing that you will always receive what you need when you need it.

For those of you who are still on the fully 3D side of the fence and not yet willing to accept things like 'energy' or 'trusting the universe', I understand that this seems like a weird, frustrating, or even a foolish stance to take. I get it. A 3D mind definitely struggles with the idea of 'trusting the universe'. There's not much I can say to convince you otherwise for now, but perhaps the section of this book on Manifesting will help you understand. I will explain how acting in accordance with the rules of the 'law of attraction' is - at the most practical level - the best way for you to live your life, whether or not the law of attraction is real.

So, just hold your horses. Take this with a grain of salt for now and keep moving.

Just remember, letting go of the past and of attachment is of ultimate importance as you try to move from your old life and programming and into your new ones. The objects you keep around will keep mirroring back to you your old pains, your old personality and identity, your debilitating nostalgia, and your lack mentality. These objects are also keeping you rooted in an outdated and unhelpful version of yourself and training you to feel attached to old realities that are long gone. All of this needs to change so that you can evolve and you can start by decluttering your home.

Notes, Notes, Notes... everywhere!!!

This Mind Hack is super simple but so effective, and I'm willing to bet that some of you are already doing it in some ways with motivation posters and the like, but that you haven't fully considered how powerful it can be. Every second of every day your brain is taking in information and processing it consciously and subconsciously. You are constantly training your brain with everything you see. So... let's make sure that you're actively programming some good messages into your head as often as possible.

I recommend that you have notes with positive affirmations all over your home, your workspace, your car, wherever. Make sure that you are always conditioning your brain with positive messages that are uplifting and - where possible - uniquely relevant to you.

There is always conflict in our brains between the optimistic version of ourselves and the inner pessimist. They are always at war. Part of us wants to believe that the future is bright and taken care of, while another part of us is always insisting that everything is always going to be awful. Well... the idea behind this Mind Hack of 'Notes Everywhere' is for you to give the optimist side of you a statistical advantage. You can make sure that you tip the odds in your favor in terms of having a positive mindset by having positive guidance for yourself all around.

Here are just some of the messages that I have up in my place, that I see every single day:

- Fear is always an illusion.
- Learn TRUE patience.
- Love your challenges.
- It's all a game (I have this one on the inside of my front door, so that I see it every time I step out into the real world. It's a reminder not to take things too seriously).
- It will all happen at once (this one is to remind myself not to get down on myself if I don't see progress in my life as quickly as I want to).
- More release = More abundance.
- Master transformer (referring to my ability to guide people towards their own transformations).
- Focus on the moment.
- The outcome is certain.
- And many more...

These notes have multiple purposes. On the one hand, every time you consciously notice them you repeat those phrases in your head and - just like the affirmations you were working on earlier - they help to pave certain pathways. A bonus is that even when you don't consciously pay attention to these notes, whenever your eyes move over them, your subconscious mind processes them, thereby paving the positive pathways at a subconscious level without any effort.

Additionally, in moments when you're struggling you will have the notes there to help support you. The positive messages will be uplifting and give you some motivation, but... far more importantly, they will help remind you of the positive mind-frame you were in when you wrote them. In general, when you write these affirmations the first time around it is because you are in an emotional space where that phrase resonates with you, and being able to recall that feeling later on is very helpful.

For example, I actually have several notes that say things like "fear is always an illusion" or "you have nothing to worry about ever". I wrote those notes in moments when I was feeling really good, truly connected to the universe, and truly certain that - even through the dark times - I am always moving in the right direction. Now, when I do start stressing out and I see these notes, it's not just that the uplifting slogans can help motivate me at the conscious level, but the notes help me connect with the emotions and the real sense of fearlessness that I had when I wrote those words in the first place. They remind me that I possess that fearlessness inside of me, and that the instance of stress and worry that I'm feeling at that moment is just an illusion. It reminds me of a version of myself that knows - beyond the shadow of a doubt - that I have nothing to fear, and that brings me back into the vibration of self-assurance, trust, and faith that I was in when I wrote the note in the first place.

These written notes work on various levels and they are so easy to make and to use. It's basically just foolish not to.

When you invoke this practice, I suggest not just writing your notes in pen on a post-it. If you do, you'll really have to be right up close to see it, and in general it will only register at a superficial level because you will have to focus more on the post-it for your eyes to have enough time to register the message.

Instead, I suggest getting some white index cards and writing your messages on them with a black Sharpie (magic marker). Make sure that you can read them from 10 feet away. That way, even when you don't notice them consciously, your brain will have registered them, and every time you register the messages you shoot neurons down certain pathways that are helping to program those messages into your mind and make them more of a natural 'go-to' option. You want your brain to start defaulting to the frequency of these positive messages whenever it loses focus or gets triggered into auto-pilot mode.

Use whatever positive affirmations you might have seen around that resonate with you, and if any phrases ever pop into your head on their own, then you should definitely use those. Every once in a while, you'll have a revelation about your own life and your own healing, and those are things that you should absolutely write down and have pinned around. You're always working on yourself, and new phrases regarding brilliant 'a-ha! moments' will pop into your head all the time. Pay attention to them and write them down. These phrases and lessons often have more significance than you realize. Oftentimes, six months after writing one of them down, you'll see that message at the exact time that you need it, and it will feel like your future-self left you that message in advance for the exact time that you will have needed it.

That's just extra-reassuring and amusing when it happens.

The bonus of seeing these 'time-travel messages' that you divined for yourself is that it will help connect you to higher consciousness. It really helps you see things from a higher, 'divine timing and guidance' kind of perspective and connects you to a view of the universe where there is more than just the physical world you see around you. It will help you open up more and more a larger understanding of the universe, and to the next topic that we need to discuss...

8

Accept the 'Supernatural'

At its core, this whole emotional healing journey that we are on is about eliminating fear. Fear is at the root of all of our anger, jealousy, regret, worry, and overall suffering. We are afraid of feeling the emotions associated with our past traumas. We are afraid of what might or might not happen if we express ourselves or follow our own paths. We are afraid of all the things that could go wrong in our lives and all the things that people might think about us, and it is because of this fear that we live a life that is inauthentic to ourselves in a way that keeps us betraying ourselves and perpetuating our own pain.

What we are truly seeking is a life without fear where we can let go, fully be and express ourselves and where we can follow whatever path the universe lights up for us along the way.

Through emotional healing - by developing the emotional skills to handle anything that comes up and to face your uncomfortable and unresolved trauma without resistance or worry - you will begin to eliminate fear. You will realize that all of the uncomfortable things that you were running from inside of yourself never truly had the power to hurt you in the first place. You will recognize the illusion behind most of your suffering and all of the reasons why you don't need to carry this pain with you anymore. You will learn that the only real problem is how you feel about what's happening in your life, not so much the thing that's happening itself.

Still though, there are sometimes limits to how far that kind of conscious reasoning can take you.

No matter how emotionally strong you get, there are still going to be times when uncertainty creeps in and fear might start to rise. You might recognize and realize your own self-harming cycles but you will still wonder about the outcomes of your decisions and stress about the direction of your life or the meaning of it all. It is in these moments that you need to add one extra piece to the puzzle. A piece which, for many - including myself - is a really difficult concept to accept in the beginning, and that is 'faith'.

Faith was not something that came naturally to me for most of my life. As a child, I believed in God, but by 12 years old I was already questioning my religion and from that point on, any element of faith was slowly squeezed out of me.

What I eventually realized, though, was that faith without science is nonsense, and science without faith is meaningless. The two truly do go hand-in-hand and there is no conflict between them when we can understand the breadth and limits of each one respectively. We only see conflict between Science and Spirit because we have been looking at things in an overly simplistic, black and white, dualistic way where everything must either 'Be or Not Be'. We have trained ourselves to think that only one view about anything may be accurate and that there is no room for multiple perspectives on a 'fact'. Something either is or isn't the case, and that's all there is to it.

This is, however, a multi-dimensional universe that is not limited to the realms of space and time or to the restricted reasoning of duality. The physical world is but one element of the fullness of reality. There are things in this universe that our five primary senses and our physical bodies are simply not connected with, and just about everything in this universe exists in multiple states at the same time. In order to reach the next stage of our personal and collective evolutions, we are going to need to start developing some level of faith in things that we can't see, prove, or demonstrate in a measurable and quantifiable way (yet... at least).

You can view the word 'faith' however you want to, here. For the religious among you, great. You already have a framework and a starting point. For those of you who are more resistant, though, I have good news! We are NOT talking about faith in 'God' necessarily, certainly not faith in 'religion', and not even faith in any kind of 'higher power' or mystical beings or anything like that. All of those can certainly fit into the notion of faith that we're moving towards, but they aren't at all the core concept of what we are talking about. They aren't necessary.

Personally, I don't believe in 'God' in the traditional sense. Although, more and more, as I find myself talking about 'the Universe', I continually ask myself 'what's the difference?' Do I actually believe in 'God' and am just uncomfortable with the word? Maybe. Although... I believe there's a certain element of cognition and intentionality associated with the word 'God' that we don't need to attach to a more esoteric concept like 'The Universe', but maybe we're just splitting hairs now? Six of one, half a dozen of the other?

Nonetheless, you certainly don't need to have faith in 'God' in order to muster up the level and kind of faith that we are talking about here.

All we are truly talking about - and all I really mean when I refer to the concepts of 'faith' and 'spirituality' - is a recognition of the fact that we and the universe actually consist of more than what exists on the physical plane. We exist in other dimensions... or to put it more simply, in other 'ways'... than we have been traditionally taught that we do. We have been examining the physical world so much and basing our existence on that element of ourselves that we have completely forgotten that there is more to us than our physical bodies.

For example, emotions are not something that can be physically pointed to, although they are a real and fundamental part of our experience of reality. Traditionally, in the context of western science, we have tried to reduce emotions to a strictly physical phenomenon. We've studied the nerves and the brain and the chemicals that get released when we experience a certain emotion, etc. We can point to all of the physical mechanisms that operate in relation to emotions and we try to equate the two. Science has tried to express emotions as a strictly physical happening, but no matter what the role of dopamine is in our brains, 'dopamine' and 'the feeling of happiness' are not at all the same thing.

Happiness, joy, sadness, anger, etc. These are NOT physical things. If they exist at all - and they do (which we know for certain because we experience them) - then they exist in a dimension that is non-physical. In other words, they represent a part of our existence and our experience of reality that has no 'spatial coordinates'. Everything physical in this world must exist in a space, but emotions take up no space. So, how can we coalesce the notion of 'emotions' with a strictly physical universe?

Sure, you can point to dopamine, you can point to nerve endings, but where - may I ask - is 'happiness'? You feel it. You experience it. You thereby know that it is real, but you can't point to it and you can't truly measure it, quantify it, or show it to someone. Happiness is not something that can be located on the physical plane of existence, and yet it exists and we experience it. We need to expand our view of the universe to account for the non-physical elements of our experience of reality (and other non-physical elements that we – as humans – don't experience).

All that faith is truly about, then - at its core - is opening ourselves up to accept the reality of things that we sense and/or otherwise experience, that cannot be quantitatively observed, measured, or proven. It is the recognition that something does not need to be objectively or demonstrably measurable through our current science and technology in order to be real. There are plenty of aspects of our experience of life and reality that cannot be truly translated out of our own experience and communicated to others and/or proven to them, and that are therefore unexaminable scientifically.

There is - for example - an age-old question of whether or not the color that I see as 'blue' is actually the same color that you see as 'blue'. It might very well be the case that the color that I believe to be blue is the color that you believe to be green, but throughout our lifetimes we were each taught that 'the color of the sky is blue'. So, although we are both experiencing a different sensation, we have trained ourselves to call it the same thing. We both call the color of the sky 'blue' even though we are both seeing a different color.

Point being, we cannot possibly communicate to one another the fundamental aspects and qualities of our sensory experience. It is fundamentally and literally impossible to do so. Our inner world cannot possibly be translated and communicated to anyone outside of our own heads, and yet, to ignore the reality and the relevance of our inner experiences is truly foolish.

To wait for someone else to justify our experience of reality is unwise, and - unfortunately - it's the sleeping/auto-pilot state most of us have been in our whole lives. We were trained and taught not to bother analyzing our own inner experiences too much specifically BECAUSE they couldn't be demonstrably shown to and quantifiably measured by others. We were trained to think that any subjective experience is irrelevant to reality because it can't be proven or measured, and if it can't be proven or measured then it's not real. This is the limitation that we need to break through.

You need to start opening up your mind to the notion that your inner experiences, even the ones that seem to defy your physical conceptions of the world, are - or at least can be - representative of real truth. Remember, science is not a 'thing', it is a method. It is a way of interpreting and analyzing data. If you begin applying the scientific method to your own inner data of your experience of life (data that, by its nature, cannot be measured, communicated, or expressed, but can only be tallied and gathered internally by yourself), you will start to see that you have access to more truths about the nature of the universe than you thought you did.

What I mean when I say the word 'faith' then, is largely just about trusting your inner experiences. I mean that you need to start recognizing the validity of things that you experience that cannot be measured and shown to others. When you can start accepting these kinds of things, you can open yourself up to a larger conception of who you are and how the universe works.

Out of body experiences, near death experiences, premonitions, extra-sensory experiences, encounters with spirits, visions, sudden awakenings, kundalini, chi, prana, auras, etc. These are all things that countless people through all cultures and times have been experiencing, and when we are able to look at our universe through a multi-dimensional, quantum lens they actually make perfect sense. It's just that if we look at things through a strictly Newtonian lens, they seem completely insane and ridiculous. Your inner experiences that can't be measured are your key to a higher conception of the universe, and you need to have enough faith in yourself to trust that your experiences are legitimate.

It has taken humanity a certain amount of time to be able to understand our reality from a higher perspective like this, and that's a big part of what this whole 'awakening' that is happening on this earth right now revolves around. We are evolving to a higher perspective and understanding about who we truly are and how the universe functions. We are gaining a higher dimensional understanding of our role in the universe through advancements in quantum mechanics.

Some of the greatest minds in our world (including Albert Einstein and Nikola Tesla) already knew and understood this concept, but it's simply taken the rest of us a while to catch up. We need to be able to look at the universe through a lens that isn't so black and white and limited to the dimensions of space and time. There are more dimensions. There is more to analyze and more to experience than we previously believed.

My favorite quote from Shakespeare is "There are more things in heaven and Earth, Horatio, Than are dreamt of in your philosophy", and this is the mindset we need to adapt. There is more to our universe than what most of us have bothered to consider just yet, and when we open ourselves up to a higher dimensional understanding of how the universe functions, we will be able to free ourselves more fully and more effectively from the fear that has been keeping us prisoner in our own lives.

Think about it like a two dimensional stick figure suddenly realizing that there is actually a third dimension, and having that two dimensional figure popping off the piece of paper to suddenly develop depth and experience an extra dimension of reality. That extra dimension was there the whole time, but a stick figure is incapable of experiencing or understanding it. From a higher third dimension though, far more is possible than was available to the stick figure before this evolution and expansion. A two-dimensional mind cannot possibly conceive of what a third dimension looks like, but that doesn't mean that a third 'higher' dimension doesn't exist.

At the physical level, we are three dimensional beings traveling through the fourth dimension of time. We know that higher dimensions exist and we can represent them mathematically, but the human mind is literally incapable of envisioning a fourth dimensional object. We know mathematically that they exist, but a three dimensional mind cannot possibly envision it. We can only do our best to create three dimensional representations of how a fourth dimension relates to our reality. We know this now, but most people haven't yet wrapped their heads around it or spent any time thinking about it.

Being able to see things from a higher perspective like this is important, though, when you get lost in the uncertainty and confusion of your human life. It can help remind you that - from this higher perspective - you know that everything is actually ok. You know that you are only seeing a small portion of what is happening in your life, and you can maintain a level of faith that whatever you are going through in the moment is going to lead you to wherever you need to be, even if it takes you a while to find out how.

The more that you can recognize that the limits of your old perspectives are illusions, the more that you can let go, surrender, and relax into the experience of whatever is happening in your life at the moment. Understanding that you only have a very limited view of what is happening in your life makes your experience of life a little more like watching a movie. Even in the dark moments, you don't get too scared because you know that it's all an illusion anyway and that everything turns out ok. Even if the movie is a tragedy, it is what it's meant to be.

A recognition that you are actually more than your physical body and a development of this 'faith' muscle is the last piece of the puzzle to helping you release fear in the moments when plain old emotional mastery fails to overcome an instantaneous, uncomfortable emotion or thought.

Developing faith is how you conquer the last bits of fear that you are holding on to.

'Ok... even if this is true, you can't actively choose to develop faith... can you?'

Well... in a traditional sense... no. You can't just choose to start believing in God and angels all of a sudden at a conscious level. You can't just flip a switch and decide one day that those kinds of things exist in your reality - if they didn't a day ago and if they contradict other things that you believe. You can't just magically coalesce your scientific beliefs and your spiritual ones in an instant without some deeper investigation. You can't choose to start believing in higher dimensions any more than you can choose to love some food that you actually hate.

What you can do, though, is merely stop resisting these concepts so intently (which you're actually just doing because you are afraid and insecure about challenging your already strongly formed beliefs) and start seeking out knowledge about new things. You can release your resistance to concepts that challenge your physical view of the universe and begin to open up to things you didn't understand before.

You can begin to wrap your head around the idea that you don't know half as much as you think you did and you can begin to be ok with the idea that you have a lot more to learn about your universe. It is only from fear and arrogance that we refuse to do this. We are afraid to admit that we have been living our lives based on lies and misunderstandings.

This is actually one of the most challenging parts of 'awakening'. There is a lot of shame and guilt involved when you start recognizing all of the ways that you so belligerently tried to force others to believe what you believed and to act in ways that were so obviously correct to you at the time - but were actually based on a limited and inaccurate view of the world. It's incredibly uncomfortable to admit that you were wrong about the most fundamental elements of your belief systems. In particular for parents, who spent their lives programming their beliefs into their kids. It is extremely uncomfortable and unpleasant to start recognizing and taking responsibility for all of the ways you caused pain to yourself and to others by insisting on things that you are now realizing were mistaken.

I get it. I've been there. If you want to achieve inner peace and the next level of your life and evolution, though, this is exactly what needs to happen. You will need to let down your defenses for long enough to accept and admit that you don't know squat, and that so much that you used to insist was impossible and insane is actually true. One big lesson that I learned for myself through my awakening was, 'just because it's insane doesn't mean it's not true'. You are going to need to let go of the fear of admitting that and of confronting all of your false, limiting beliefs.

As you begin to release fear a little through your other healing modalities, you will start releasing your defensiveness around your 'strictly physical' belief system, you will start acknowledging the role of your emotions more, and all this will help you start opening up to ideas that used to seem strange to you. From there, it will simply be a matter of staying open minded and seeking out something that resonates with you in the realm of spirituality, and finding a source for information about the spiritual that still seems grounded enough in reality for you to accept. In other words, you'll have to find an introduction to the occult that feels ok to you, so to speak.

Feeling connected to your emotions is the bridge that can lead you to rediscover enough of yourself to open you back up to grand universal concepts, but then you'll need to find that first step into a deeper universe that you are slightly ready to accept. Maybe it's past lives, maybe it's auras, or maybe it's manifesting and the law of attraction. Whatever it is, you will need to find one small concept that used to seem impossible and strange to you, but that is somehow tugging at your heartstrings anyway. Something is out there for you. Start small, open yourself up, and see where it takes you. I can almost guarantee that you have some nagging feeling in yourself about something that seems 'out there' and that either seems intuitively right to you, or that you've had an experience with, and you need to connect to that sense of intrigue inside of you and feed it.

The first time you hear a story about someone who can see auras or remember their past lives, it seems completely insane and you roll your eyes at them and write them off as a lunatic. That's certainly what I used to do. The 5th time you hear a story like that you're laughing at these people. The 50th time, you're getting frustrated at all the idiots who believe things they can't prove and you're arrogantly self-assured about the certainty of your beliefs over theirs. But... the 500th time? The 1,000th time?

Eventually, you're forced to start recognizing that it can't be the case that ALL these people are insane, right? Regular people with regular jobs and regular lives all around the world, from all races, ages, cultures, and religions all experiencing the same kinds of indescribable inner experiences in complete isolation from one another. Most of these people simply don't speak about their experiences because they know people will think they are crazy, but more people than you imagine - most likely your own friends and family - have had these experiences and either don't talk about them or just wrote them off, telling themselves that they were imagining it as well.

When they tried expressing these crazy experiences to others, they were called crazy, and so they just put the experience aside and moved on. It might simply be the case that their experiences contradicted their own beliefs so fundamentally that they never told anyone because they themselves thought that they were just going crazy. Most of us have actually had some kind of spiritual experiences, but since we couldn't understand the spiritual aspect of them from within our scientific view of the world (like a 2-dimensional figure trying to understand the movements of a 3-dimensional person) we just put them aside, pretended they never happened or that we imagined them, and moved on. The universe tried to wake us up, but we weren't ready and we went back to sleep.

I have a friend I have known for almost 20 years now, and it wasn't until I started going through my own spiritual awakening a few years ago that she revealed to me that she actually has a memory of being on 'the other side', before this lifetime, actively choosing her body and some of the experiences and lessons that she wanted to learn and experiment with in this life. She always had that memory with her but it simply never came up in conversation. She doesn't live her life according to these principles. She is not 'spiritual' in any practical way. She doesn't act crazy or woo-woo. She is an intelligent, educated, practical, and successful person living the corporate life, and I've known her for more than half of my life, never knowing that she had this memory.

I'm willing to bet that you know people like this as well. We just don't talk about things that make us vulnerable to criticism or that force us to start reconciling our own conflicting beliefs. Most people just don't spend enough time truly investigating the universe or their experience of reality enough to bother needing answers, so it's easy for them to just ignore these things and live out their human lives.

I also worked with an amazing and talented woman at a restaurant who told me that she could see auras (I've heard that from hundreds of people by now), and I was friends for a while with a woman who told me that she had been able to astral travel since she was young. These are regular people. Both of them are incredibly talented, intelligent and not living their lives in any overtly spiritual ways. The one who tells me that she astral travels regularly is a cancer researcher, and the one who sees auras is a brilliantly talented photographer. They are regular people living their lives without any sign of spirituality from the outside, who nonetheless live with these deeply spiritual experiences as a 'matter of fact' part of their reality. They just don't talk about it most of the time unless it comes up that you're on the same page.

The one who sees auras - for example - only revealed this because I happened to make a joke about my (not serious) theory that cats are actually reincarnated humans and that that's why they are so rude to their human owners most of the time. I joked that cats remember being human and therefore have a level of disdain for us, and that led us to talking about past lives and the extra senses that animals sometimes seem to have. This led her to open up about her ability to see auras. Point being, it was only a very random circumstantial occurrence that led to us discovering our shared spiritual beliefs, and were it not for my joke about cats we never would have discovered it, and if we weren't both on the same page spiritually already the conversation wouldn't have evolved in that direction. These experiences stay buried and undiscussed most of the time.

Again... I know that something like seeing auras or astral projection sounds completely insane when you first start trying to wrap your head around it, but I challenge you to go on YouTube right now and search up 'how to astral travel'. Check out the vast amounts of people talking about it, and see if they all just seem like ultra-spiritual crazy loons to you, or if - maybe even just some of them - seem like regular people who have just experienced something that you haven't. I promise you; you will find regular, intelligent, well-spoken people without ties to any religion or belief system who will tell you about their weird experiences in the astral realm.

Then go on Amazon and search up books on astral travel. See the plethora of books out there on the subject. Then research the Monroe Institute. Then look up subjects like 'hemi sync', 'the gateway experience', and 'remote viewing'. At a certain point, the evidence becomes overwhelming and you're forced to at least start wondering whether you've been blocking yourself off from universal truths your whole life. From that point, it will take your brain some time to start accepting this stuff. It won't happen instantly, but if you do this right now you will open the doors for yourself to start moving in the direction of faith and wonder.

The thing that finally put me over the edge was a book called 'Psychic Warrior' by David Morehouse. Not a phenomenal book by any means, but it just so happened to come into my life to be the straw that broke the camel's back for me about believing in the 'supernatural'.

David Morehouse was a military man who was recruited by the CIA for their 'Psychic Spy' program in the 1980's, where they were trained in remote viewing in order to gather intel on enemy operations. In the book, he talks about traveling beyond the realms of space and time through astral travel practices that gave him access to higher dimensions. He is well aware of how insane it is, by the way, and much of the book is about the psychological trauma he endured trying to open up to this stuff and make sense of it... (I couldn't help but think - as I read the book - that he should have taken my emotional mastery course before diving into that world!)

It is largely because of that element of the book - his psychological and emotional struggles of coming to grips with the reality of what he was trained to do - that allowed me to believe it. I needed to hear that he was equally as confused and taken aback by this as anyone else would be. If he had just spoken as if it was all obvious, I might have written the whole thing off as just another tall tale, but because the focus of the book was actually about how these experiences tore his life apart - I was able to relate, understand, and believe.

In the very first chapter of the book, he recounts his experience of getting to talk to his dead friend who disappeared in a helicopter crash during a classified mission. David never got to find out what happened to his friend, and when he was recruited into this special unit, he brought it up with a superior officer who helped him find his dead friend on the astral plane, find out what happened, and say his goodbyes.

For me, hearing an old-school military man - the last kind of person you would ever expect to talk about emotions or spiritual matters - confess his experiences in such a 'matter-of-fact' way, allowed me to finally let my guard down about this stuff and truly accept it. In the book, he also mentions how his dad eventually revealed to him that he too had experiences with 'an angel' throughout his life, going back to reinforce my earlier statement that you probably already know people who have had these insane experiences and just never talk about them. Start opening up about this stuff and see what people have to say. You might be surprised!

[For the record... I've also spoken to people who still tell foolish or tall tales about things they think to be 'supernatural' that aren't, and I know a LOT of spiritual people who like to overly-spiritualize absolutely everything they experience. I'm not saying to open up to gullibility and just accept everything you hear. There are indeed still foolish people out there who have mistakes and misunderstandings about their own experiences.

I'm also aware that this argument of 'look at all the regular people who believe this stuff' could be used to support religion or conspiracy theories in other contexts. I'm aware that this isn't conclusive logic or argumentation to 'prove' anything one way or another. I'm just saying... open up your understanding of the universe, and start looking at things from a different angle. Be open... but don't be a fool.

There is a tendency to get overly swept up in a spiritual understanding of the world when you first discover it. We do tend to go a little too far when we first open up to these things. I certainly had a hard time finding a balance for a while, and even slipped into some conspiracy stuff briefly. So, you do have to be careful. But... just stay open and find a balance. Learn to investigate and take your inner experiences more seriously, and hear people out about their own inner experiences, then make up your mind.]

It was probably two and a half years in between when I first heard about 'remote viewing' and when I was finally able to accept it as truth, but once I did... I knew even more deeply that I had nothing to fear ever again in this lifetime, because I now know that even death isn't what we think it is. If David Morehouse was able to find and speak to his friend after his passing, then clearly that person's spirit lives on beyond the dimensions of space and time. This knowledge has allowed me to relax more about my identity and my place in this world, and to let go of a lot of attachments, expectations, and desires. I am much more able to see myself as both a passenger and a driver in my own life, finding a balance between what I can control and know, and what I can't.

This perspective is so much more freeing than you might realize.

> A life with faith is a life without fear, and that is the life most worth living.

Start opening yourself up. Opening up to the supernatural is a Mind Hack that will break your reality wide open, and it starts by simply letting go of resistance. Drop the fear around admitting and realizing that your adamant beliefs about how the universe functions at the physical level are but one small part of what is really happening all around you, and try and wrap your mind around multiple dimensions. Physics is real. Physical reality is real... but there are elements of reality that aren't physical, as well. Just because something does not exist on or interact with the physical realm, does not mean that it's not real.

Allow yourself the space to start investigating things that seem weird and see where it takes you.

9

Frequency Manipulation

There are five primary types of brain states or frequency ranges that we can operate in at any given time; delta, theta, gamma, alpha, and beta. Each one of these frequencies relates to a different state of consciousness or awareness. Alpha, for example, refers to a state of deep relaxation while being awake and conscious, whereas while we move into a true sleep state, theta waves begin to rise and become the prominent frequency.

Without getting too much into the science of it, because frankly I'm not qualified to truly explain it, I'd like to share with you two simple tools that you can use to hack the frequency of your mind and help you shift brain states to be more productive or effective in whatever you're doing. You can use these tools to help you achieve deep states of relaxation or to improve your focus. You can manipulate your brain into getting into the flow you want it to be in.

A - Solfeggio Frequencies.

I find it truly fascinating how some concepts can seem so ancient, esoteric, and 'out of left field' insane on the one hand, while simultaneously seeming like scientifically advanced futuristic tech on the other. There are times when the line between 'magic' and 'science' gets blurred and the mind can't decide which of the two it's dealing with.

Solfeggio frequencies are one of these concepts.

The reason that they can seem both mystical and modern is because they originated in times of old - having been used by monks in their meditations - but we use modern technology to create the most effective versions of these tones and frequencies - and we do it with a scientific understanding of how these frequencies work. The monks who developed these methods didn't know, understand, or care about what we may call 'the science of the matter'. They weren't concerned with measuring brain states and interpreting frequency, and yet they were intuitively aware of something that we - in modern society - are too disconnected from our feelings to be able to sense most of the time. They knew intuitively what took us a very long time to understand intellectually.

Additionally, the scientifically minded amongst us will meet some intellectual resistance when we try understanding some ancient technique developed by monks, and yet... despite our rational resistance to something that seems so 'out there', these solfeggio frequencies are exactly what you will hear playing in the background at any good spa you walk into, covered by the sounds of harps. In that kind of a setting, you will hear these dulcet tones and intuitively know that these sounds induce a state of relaxation, but... take a modern skeptic out of the spa and try telling them about solfeggio frequencies that monks used for meditation and they will look at you like a quack, and write you off as a nutcase.

Trust me... I've tried.

These frequencies and the way that we use them are scientifically advanced, even though they originate from ancient esoteric practices that irk our intellectual minds... until we come to understand them.

The principle behind Solfeggio frequencies is very simple, though. By playing sounds of a certain frequency, we help can shift the brain into a particular frequency of our choice, to help achieve states of relaxation, inspiration, deep sleep, deep focus, or of healing. There is nothing mystical or weird about this. It's a matter of getting into 'flow states' or simply getting into the right headspace for whatever it is that you are trying to accomplish. It's a matter of training your brain to be in the right gear at all times.

There are six primary solfeggio frequencies that resonate with different states of consciousness and different emotions. The frequency of 528hz, for example, is associated with emotional alertness, physical healing and DNA repair while the frequency of 741hz can help us tap into our intuition to solve problems and express solutions. I won't bother listing all of the frequencies here, but I'll point out that the original list of six frequencies that were used by monks has been widely expanded, and now you can search up frequencies for all kinds of things, from weight loss to astral projection and lucid dreaming.

Now, as for the efficacy of these frequencies... How well do they work? Where are the studies?

If you are to do your own research on this matter through scientific studies alone, you'll find that the results are - at best - questionable and mostly not truly in support of their demonstrable scientific efficacy. I truly believe, however, that - as it is with all spiritual concepts - the issue is that these concepts are being misunderstood, misinterpreted, and measured in ways that cannot possibly truly quantify and demonstrate what is really happening.

Scientifically-minded people who hear the claims of the spiritually-minded about these topics tend to think that something like a solfeggio frequency is meant to be a 'miracle cure'. They hear spiritual people talking about the powers of frequency to heal you, and they think that the spiritual person means that you can play these frequencies and that the sounds themselves will heal you.

Based on that, the scientifically-minded person decides to perform an experiment, and they believe that if you take a frequency that is meant to help you heal, play it to a cancer patient, and their tumor doesn't shrink, that the whole concept of solfeggio frequencies is nonsense, and they throw out the baby with the bathwater.

To those who truly understand solfeggio frequencies and other spiritual healing modalities properly, though, it is never believed that this is how they would work.

The frequency is not meant to have a direct impact at the physical level. It was never presumed that these frequencies were something that you could shoot at a tumor or broken leg, that will then instruct the atoms of your body to restructure themselves for health. Of course, if that's what you believe a spiritual person is saying when they tell you that solfeggio frequencies can help you heal, you would be right to roll your eyes and walk away.

That's not the intention, though.

Remember, this is a frequency hack. We are trying to use these frequencies to help us achieve a certain brain state that can be accessed to help our brains and our bodies perform a certain function. So, the frequency itself is never going to help you heal. Being in a relaxed brain state, however - where your brain and body can focus on performing a certain task - can, and that is precisely what we are trying to accomplish. Basically, there is a certain brain state from which your body can perform its function of self-repair more efficiently, and we want to access that state (or other states).

Using solfeggio frequencies, then, much like hypnosis - requires that you actively participate in the process. Someone who is actively resisting a hypnotist is incredibly unlikely to be hypnotized, and the same goes for guided meditation, solfeggio frequencies, or any other kind of induced relaxation. You have to allow the process to happen and take part in it. It is a tool that you can use and nothing more. A hammer does nothing if there is not a craftsman there actively and intentionally wielding it, nor do solfeggio frequencies.

That's what a lot of scientists are doing when they are trying to debunk spiritual practices. They are removing the core of what the practice is by looking at it strictly numerically, without the real conscious content behind it. They look at a hammer without a craftsman and say "Look! The hammer didn't build a house! Hammers are useless spiritual nonsense!". Then they walk away acting all smug because they are scientists and you are a luddite.

We all know that the brain and the human body are capable of doing miraculous things, shocking even doctors with mind-blowing health recoveries that are inexplicable, all the time. Using tools like solfeggio frequencies to intentionally shift our brain states is just a way that we can tap into more of our minds' and bodies' internal untapped potential. It takes practice, work and active participation though. So, no... just playing solfeggio frequencies isn't going to have any effect if your goal is to debunk them.

If you perform a scientific study with a group of skeptics who are sitting there listening to these sounds, all the while thinking, 'this is nonsense and I feel like a fool... when can I go get lunch?', or 'yes please... heal my cancer... I'll take anything, please just blast these frequencies into my tumors', of course you are going to end up with less than encouraging results. If you run the experiment on the direct physical effects of these sounds on the human body, you won't see anything.

(Side note... there are actually sound waves that have been shown to reduce the size of tumors in cancer patients, and the spiritual community is waiting for the rest of the world to open their minds to these kinds of sound and light based healing techniques. But, that is not the same as solfeggio frequencies. That is not what we are talking about here. Those are two entirely different topics.)

If you practice using these frequencies to help you achieve a state of focused and intentional relaxation, though, and if you practice other forms of mental mastery to help control the body and encourage it to accelerate its own miraculous healing potential, then a lot can be done using tools like this. Helping you alleviate anxiety and stress is one of the more simple and obvious examples. These are incredibly soothing tones - if nothing else - and that's why they are used in spas.

If you don't yet believe that the human mind can perform miracles that help you exceed the limitations of what you typically think the human body can achieve - for increased functioning and great healing - I suggest you look up Wim Hof, who the world has affectionately dubbed the Ice Man. He is not unique in using mental mastery to push his body to great limits, but he is certainly one of the more famous amongst them. Wim Hof uses breathwork and meditation techniques to prime his body for extremely cold temperatures, sitting in ice baths as if he were relaxing in a sauna.

Recognizing the immense capacities of the human body and mind and how 'easily' they can be trained to do the miraculous is part of the grand awakening we are collectively going through right now. The feeble limitations of the human form that we believed to be ruling us are fading away slightly and we are opening up our minds to greater possibilities.

We are evolving.

Solfeggio frequencies are easy to find. Just head to YouTube, type in 'solfeggio' and start experimenting with whichever ones resonate with you at the time. If you're stressed and anxious - for example - just scroll through a few of them until one of them feels good to you. Don't worry about the classification of which frequency is meant to have which result. Especially when you're starting, just go with what feels right.

Of course, you absolutely can just look up 'solfeggio for anxiety', or anything like that, and you'll find plenty of options.

For many of you, you might pop on these frequencies to help you relax and - at the start - they might make you even more anxious and frustrated than before you put them on. This is completely normal and natural if you are in a state of extreme resistance, fear, anger, anxiety, etc. Even, and especially, if you're **so** stuck in that energy that you can't even notice and recognize that you're in it. The solfeggio sounds that you hear carry the frequency of a particular emotion or state of consciousness, and when you are in the exact opposite state of consciousness that the frequency is trying to help induce, this is going to cause even more cognitive dissonance and it will exacerbate the negative feelings that you are having, in that moment. It will be uncomfortable, the way that giving love to someone who truly hates themselves is uncomfortable for that person.

That is just part of the transition process though. It takes time for the brain to adjust to this new state. You don't just pop on the sound and your brain instantaneously flips a switch. It's more like when you bring a fish home from the pet store. You have the fish in a bag of water, and before just dumping the fish into your own tank, you need to put the whole bag into the tank and let the temperature of the water in the bag slowly adjust to the temperature of the tank.

This is precisely what you are doing with your brain. You are taking your brain, which is operating at a particular frequency right now, and surrounding it with a frequency of a different nature, so that it can slowly adjust and adapt to its new environment. If you actively participate in this process (if you actively try to get yourself in tune with the vibration of the solfeggio frequency that you are listening to by focusing on it and truly sitting with it), if you actively calm your mind, and actively focus on these sounds, then over time you will move your brain from its state of fear, panic, and alertness, and into a state of comfort, safety and relaxation.

It takes practice to learn how to do this, of course. Emotional mastery doesn't happen in an instant, even with tools like this. You can start practicing, though, because emotional mastery is something you want to achieve and because you don't want to suffer anymore, and over time you'll get better at shifting your brain into these states intentionally, much more quickly. Again... It is a process and a practice. Not a miracle cure.

You're trying to shift into the vibration and frequency of calm, relaxed, love, and Solfeggio frequencies are a tool that you can use to manipulate your brain in that direction. Nothing more.

B - Binaural Beats

Binaural beats are basically the levelled up older brother of solfeggio frequencies. They have a slightly loftier goal in mind and use more advanced and scientifically backed technology, but overall they fall under the same category of 'frequency manipulation'. The ultimate goal of Binaural Beats are not only to shift our brain towards states of particular functions (like healing, creativity, relaxation or alertness), but also to help us achieve a state known as 'hemi-sync' (otherwise known as 'brain hemisphere synchronization'), which - in common parlance - is simply a state where the left and right hemispheres of the brain are operating in a state of harmony. Most of the time, the left sides of our brains have priority and take up more energy, but putting our brains into a state of balance and hemi-sync can have mind-blowing uses and effects, like (for example) achieving astral travel, out of body experiences, and remote viewing.

Hemi-sync is something discussed by David Morehouse in his adventures in 'Physic Warrior', and in fact, if you go to Google right now and type "CIA and hemisync" you will see a link to a document released directly on the CIA website through the freedom of information act that discusses what is known as the 'Gateway Process', which *"is a training system designed to bring enhanced strength, focus and coherence to the amplitude and frequency of brainwave output between the left and right hemispheres so as to alter consciousness, moving it outside the physical sphere so as to ultimately escape even the restrictions of time and space. The participant then gains access to the various levels of intuitive knowledge which the universe offers."*

(The actual title of the article is 'Analysis and assessment of Gateway Process', and - at the time of this writing - it can be found here: https://www.cia.gov/readingroom/docs/CIA-RDP96-00788R001700210016-5.pdf)

Yes... those words about the 'intuitive knowledge which the universe offers' and 'escaping the limits of space and time' were written by Wayne M Mcdonnel, a military Commander, in an official military/CIA report in which he was tasked with studying the Gateway Process back in the 80's, which means that for the last 40 years - at least - the US government, at an institutional level, was aware of and believed in the reality of extra dimensions beyond the physical and temporal ones, and the idea that we do in fact have access to them through altered consciousness techniques.

The article goes on to mention that they have had the ability to communicate with conscious beings of higher dimensions by using these practices as well.

Science fiction... eat your heart out! Reality has you beat.

Binaural beats work by pumping two similar but different frequencies into the left and right ears. The conscious brain cannot process the two different frequencies independently at the same time, and so it attempts to process them as a singular experience, forcing the frequencies of the left and right brain to try and find a sense of equilibrium. It nudges each side of the brain closer to the frequency of the other side, moving you into this esoteric state of hemi-sync. Learning how to fully do this takes years of practice, though. Most people can't achieve such a high-end state of hemisphere synchronization easily. Much as it is with the solfeggio frequencies, Binaural Beats are a tool that you can use to amplify your practices, but you can't just shift yourself into a world of magic and universal knowledge if you are using them passively and untrained, so again... treat this as a practice.

You can find Binaural Beats easily on YouTube as well, but be aware that great binaural beats require a little more in terms of the sophistication of the soundwaves than solfeggio frequencies do. With solfeggio frequencies, it's just about the tones, so as long as you are hearing them, they can help you move your brain in a direction. Binaural beats, however, need to be more precise to have their desired impact. This means that the audio compression system used by YouTube and other online sites will generally distort and reduce the effectiveness of the sound files that were initially uploaded and they won't be as effective.

If you would like to try Binaural Beats at their best, I suggest a site called iDoser that uses scientifically designed and studied frequencies with the highest quality audio conversion to ensure the best results. Also, know that you will need to use headphones or earphones. They need to be pumped in directly to each ear. IDoser has a wide range of binaural beats for all kinds of different purposes, including the ability to mimic the effects that certain drugs will have on the brain. You can find binaural beats based on the frequency of heroin or ecstasy, or you can find others to help you access states of intense productivity or deep sleep. The choice is yours!

The possibilities are practically endless and we are learning more about these methods all the time. There is a lot of potential for real magic in our lives as we head into this new awakened world, accept the full potential of our minds, and develop technologies to help us tap into them. A lot of these technologies and techniques - like hemi-sync and the gateway experience, for example - have already been around for a long time and most of us just didn't know about them. Who knows what other wonders we've already discovered but weren't ready to wrap our heads around?! There is still so much to be discovered in our lives.

I, personally, have not yet mastered any of these techniques and have not managed to have out of body experiences or stuff like that. I also haven't really put any time into trying though, because I'm simply not there yet. It's just not my priority at this stage in my life. But I am truly excited and filled with a sense of wonder and amazement about the things I will get to explore and dive into when I reach the right stage. Right now, my focus is on keeping my head in this reality and helping people heal. Once I have my life's purpose of helping people heal running a little more on auto-pilot, I'll feel freer and more encouraged to dive into these deep esoteric concepts. For now, it's enough for me to know that they exist and that I will have the rest of my life to explore a much more expansive version of reality than I used to think was real.

I actually did almost have an out of body experience once, by the way. I started leaving my body and was moving upwards, but I got scared because I wasn't prepared for it and I came back down. I thought I was dying. I thought that if I left my body in that moment that I wouldn't come back. I was not yet so aware of the reality of astral travel, so I thought - in the moment - that if you leave, you leave. So, I stayed. It was enough, though, to help me realize that this is all real.

10

Manifesting Scripts

Many of you reading this book have certainly come across the term 'manifesting' before, but I'd say that - on average - it is still a fairly esoteric concept that your average person hasn't ever really heard of or dived into, and even those who have been studying it or practicing it for a while have a lot of misunderstandings around it, just like all of the other spiritual concepts we've been speaking about so far. Most people speak of things like this without actually knowing what they're all about. They take the spiritual and 'good-feely' aspects of a concept that promises them everything they ever wanted, without ever learning the real lessons or ideas behind them. So, I feel like it requires a bit of an explanation.

The art of Manifesting - otherwise known as/interpreted as the 'Law of Attraction' or 'reality transurfing' - is a 'spiritual' concept that basically states that you will attract into your life that which is a vibrational match for yourself. In other words, angry people will attract more anger, loving people will attract more love, those with a healthy relationship with money will attract more money whereas those who have anger and resentment towards money will stay poor.

When you are able to see things in terms of frequency, energy, and vibration as Tesla proposed, this actually makes a lot of sense. Everything is energy and similar energies will gravitate towards each other, a little like oil and water in a glass. Oil has a certain density and therefore flows to a certain position in the glass, whereas water has a different density and finds its own place. The two don't naturally mix, and neither do love and fear, or joy and anger. Those who exude the energy of love and joy at all times will find that they naturally gravitate towards people and situations that match that energy, and – of course – vice versa.

When we're thinking about this in terms of our friendships, relationships, jobs, etc..., this is actually intuitively obvious. Joyous philanthropists who spend their days at charity events (for example) will naturally find other good Samaritans to hang out with through the events and communities they frequent. Alcoholics will hang out in bars and will tend to meet and get along with other alcoholics. Spiritual people will find spiritual people, etc. This makes perfect sense to us and we can understand how these ties, connections, and decisions affect our lives in ways that create certain cycles and loops, perpetuating themselves endlessly. Who we hang out with will impact our decisions and actions, those decisions and actions will have consequences that affect our emotions and personality which will impact our choices of what to do and who to hang out with, etc. We understand how our energy can dictate our lives in that kind of way.

Law of Attraction (LoA) and Manifesting, however, go a step further and basically claim that you can create whatever you want in your life - whether it be love, money, success, talent, etc... - by attuning your energy to it first. LoA basically states that in order to attain what you want in your life; you first need to learn how to feel that way inside of yourself and that - by matching your internal energy to the vibration of the reality you want to experience - you can attract what you want into your life.

Another way of looking at it is that you can 'switch timelines' or do something known as 'reality transurfing' to move from the reality that you are currently experiencing and into another reality altogether where the thing that you want already exists and where there is a version of you that is already experiencing what you want to experience.

While we can try to make sense of this from a quantum, multi-dimensional point of view, I'd first like to point out that the beauty of learning about the law of attraction - and most of the other spiritual concepts we have been talking about - is that you don't need to understand them from a spiritual perspective in order for them to make sense. LoA and manifesting make perfect sense at the psychological level in terms of helping you get into alignment with the things that you are trying to create in your life, so that you move more and more in those directions and ultimately are able to create the experiences that you want.

We don't need to get 'spiritual' and 'mystical' about this in order for LoA and manifesting to work for us or make sense to us. So, we start practicing these spiritual kinds of things because - at some level - they just make sense psychologically or practically, and then - as we start seeing the real progress and all the deeper benefits to our new practices - we start opening up more and more to the spiritual side of things - because it just starts becoming undeniable.

We come for the science; we stay for the spirit!

Ironically though, despite that intro... I'm going to start by giving you the spiritual explanation of what manifesting is all about, and then I'll explain to you how this works out practically even if the spiritual concept is bunk.

A - The Spiritual Side

(This section is going to get a little dense in terms of metaphysics, so... feel free to skip to the next section if that's not your cup of tea.)

There are (at least) three different interpretations regarding this overall phenomenon that I have come across and they are each just a slightly different perspective on the same principle. I have mentioned them all already. They are; Manifesting, Law of Attraction, and Reality Transurfing.

Manifesting is the most 'active' of the three interpretations. The idea behind manifesting is that you and the universe are one, and that by focusing your energy and intention on a certain outcome or goal, you can literally bring that thing into existence. It is the idea that your thoughts and intentions can actually create this thing in the universe that didn't exist until you started dreaming it into existence, and that your mental and emotional intentions around this actually spawned this thing, person, or experience out of thin air. You created it with your focused intentions.

Law of Attraction is the reverse side of this, wherein it's interpreted that the thing that you are trying to bring into your life already exists in the 'ether' or - as Abraham Hicks likes to put it - the Vortex. The idea here is that all the things that you might want to have or experience already exist in an intangible form as concepts or potential realities and that by setting your own emotional dial to a certain frequency you create a kind of magnetic effect with the thing that you are trying to experience and you begin to draw it closer and closer into your actual conscious experience of reality until you meet up with it.

Lastly, Reality Transurfing is more about an infinitely multi-dimensional universe where there exists right now a version of reality where what you want is already the truth, and therefore that all you need to do is to learn how to move yourself from one timeline to another.

Whichever interpretation you choose, they all amount to the same thing - that you can control your experience of reality by attuning your vibration to be a match for the thing that you want to experience.

Yes... this all sounds completely outlandish no matter how many 'testimonials' of miraculous results you may hear. You can find stories of people who attracted great wealth, who manifested body changes or relationships, or transferred to realities where their careers had taken off, but no story is going to help you truly believe or understand this unless you experience it for yourself... and even then, probably not. No matter what I experience, I don't know if I'll ever be able to truly embody a belief in the full scope of the spiritual elements here. It's psychologically difficult from within a physical body.

One of the reasons it will always be hard to fully believe these concepts is because - even if they are true - they work much more subtly than you would generally like to think.

Presuming these laws of reality are true, you're experiencing them every day whether you realize it or not, and the main issue is simply that no-one realizes it. They are not laws that you activate by focusing on them, they are very simply the fundamental rules on which our universe is built, and you have been subject to these laws since the day you were born. When they play out, they play out in a practical and logical way that makes sense to our human minds.

They are higher dimensional truths that - when translated into our three or four dimensional reality - make sense to the human mind in a way that allows us to ignore the higher dimensional reality of what just happened. If we could see things from a fifth dimensional perspective, we could see how what ACTUALLY happened was an energetic pull between us and what we wanted, but from within our human perspective we will only be able to see the hard work that we put in to get there. It will look like normal physics and progress over time, when really the truth of the matter was something far more magical. You won't realize how you were actually steered in the direction you needed to go in by higher dimensional forces, you will only recognize the action that you took to get there. You'll think that you made the decision, when actually you were guided there by your intuition, your higher self, your soul family, spirit guides, God, or - most simply and scientifically - the higher dimensional energetic law of attraction.

We live in a 3D world and play this 3D game and most of us have been completely unaware that there are other possibilities (we were never able to consider higher dimensional causality), but - if these laws are real and true - we are finally starting to wake up to them again, giving us back the ability to take control of how we operate in relation to these laws.

It's a little bit like beginning to understand gravity. Before we understood it at all, we couldn't make sense of how birds fly or clouds float, but once we began to understand it, we were able to start manipulating our relationship with gravity to help us build blimps and airplanes. The law of gravity was always working on us, but an understanding of how it works allowed us to manipulate technology around it for our benefits.

That is what we are trying to do with the Law of Attraction. We are trying to understand a fundamental law of our universe so that we can take advantage of how it works to bring about the changes we want to see. It's not magic. It's 'meta-science'. In other words, it is a way of applying the scientific method to a higher dimensional phenomenon that can't be directly analyzed and measured through traditional physics.

Let me try to explain my conception of how these laws actually function at the 'spiritual' or 'multidimensional' level.

Think of a regular two-dimensional graph - like a stock chart. On this graph there is the 'value' axis and the 'time' axis, and there are infinite possible coordinates at which the price might be located. So, coordinates of a certain value [x value, y value] represent a certain place on this graph which represents certain qualities about the thing that we are plotting. A certain set of coordinates tells us something about the stock we are graphing - it tells us where it is on the temporal axis as well as what price it was at during that time. On this graph, there are two dimensions of coordinates. Time and value.

Ok... now let's expand the graph into four dimensions as a representation of where you are at in your life right now. There are the spatial coordinates (the three dimensions of space) and the temporal coordinates (the dimension of time), and when we plot all of those onto a four-dimensional graph we can see where exactly you are in the dimensions of space and time.[2] You would have three numbers that represent your place in three-dimensional space, and a 4th number that represents your location in time.

Following so far?

Ok, now let's imagine that the time and place of your birth is [0, 0, 0, 0] for you. It is the origin point or the center of the graph where your story on the spatial and temporal dimensions began. That is where you came into existence and you have been moving through those dimensions your whole life. So, right now you are far away from that origin point, located a vast distance from there in terms of space and time. You started at [0, 0, 0, 0] and now you are at (say) [145, 222, 444, 860]. You exist at a certain set of space-time coordinates that represent your physical and temporal location, and there are other things that exist at the same location which make up what you are currently experiencing.

Great...

Now, let's expand our understanding of ourselves and of the universe even further to include the extra dimensions that quantum mechanics requires in order to make sense of the universe. There are more than four dimensions. Space is an infinite spectrum that we vibrate in and move through, technically composed of the three

---

[2] I actually believe that time is more complex than a single 'dimension'. In the same way that space is three dimensional, I believe time to be multi-dimensional as well, but that's irrelevant here and I didn't want to confuse the matter. So... let's just look at space as the first three dimensions, and time as the 4th, as is traditionally discussed.

dimensions of length, height, and width. Time is also an infinite spectrum that we vibrate in and move through. But there are also other dimensions that we know must exist. Other infinite spectrums in which we must vibrate in and move through in order for our universe to actually make sense mathematically.

The issue is - and this is where science and spirituality diverge and need to come together - that although the mathematics of quantum mechanics require extra dimensions, pure mathematics can have no concept of what those dimensions consist of. In other words, they have quantity, but not quality. Quantum Mechanics can only tell us that there is a mathematical need for higher dimensions, but cannot conceive of what exists in those dimensions. A being that did not exist in the physical world, for example, might be able to know mathematically that there must be a 'space' dimension, but they wouldn't know anything about what 'space' actually means. It would just be a mathematical concept expressed through numbers that would not help that being understand what having a physical body meant or felt like.

So, we know mathematically that there are extra dimensions to our universe, but we don't know or understand what those dimensions are and what exists in those dimensions. Math cannot possibly tell us anything about the quality of these dimensions.

What are those extra dimensions, then? What does it even mean for there to be extra dimensions that we exist in - in a practical sense? How can we make sense of the qualitative notion of there being 'extra dimensions'? What would it be like to experience more dimensions?

My perspective is that the qualities of some of these extra dimensions are things that we actually experience all the time but simply cannot 'point to' on the spatial and temporal dimensions. Space and time are fundamental elements of our reality. They exist side by side and kind of on top of each other, but you can't point to a certain 'time' in the dimension of space, and you can't find 'space' in the dimension of time. In other words, where is 'the year 1920' on a map of the world? That's a nonsensical question because 'time' can't be expressed in terms of 'space'. The question is asking about two different dimensions. It's gibberish.

So, what other fundamental elements of our reality do we know exist, do we experience, and do we know that we can't express in terms of space and time? I believe that these elements of our reality that cannot be expressed in terms of space-time coordinates represent some of the other dimensions of the universe.

Emotion is one of these dimensions. Emotion is an infinite spectrum that we vibrate in and move through. There are no conceptual limits to the types, intensities and ranges of emotions that we could experience, and at any given moment we should be able to describe the coordinates on which we lie in the dimension of emotion. In other words, if you plotted out a graph of emotions where fear was on one end of the graph while love was on another, we would always be able to place ourselves somewhere on that graph as a representation of how we feel in that moment.

We are always capable of being located on this dimension of emotion and it is a fundamental element of our experience of reality - without which the universe as we know it would not be the same. It is something we cannot remove ourselves from, nor can we remove from our concept of the universe without changing our whole perception of what life really is. It is a spectrum on which we find ourselves constantly moving that cannot be reconciled with space and time. Emotions exist in their own spectrum. Their own dimension. We - as emotional beings - exist in that dimension in the same way that we exist in the dimensions of space and time.

Ok... So... If we exist in this dimension of emotion and if this is one of the 'higher dimensions', the question is 'how can we use that and how does that relate to Manifesting or LoA'?

I'm sure that you have all seen some science fiction time travel movie where they explain the nature of wormholes using a piece of paper. If you are standing at one point on the piece of paper and you are trying to get to a point on the opposite end of the piece of paper, then there are two ways that you can do it. You can either walk the long way along the surface of the piece of paper. Or, using your access to a higher dimension, you can fold this piece of paper over on top of itself so that the point where you are currently standing and the point you are trying to get to are actually right next to each other, and you can move through the higher dimension to get to that other point on the piece of paper instantaneously.

This is my perspective on how the LoA actually functions from a higher dimensional perspective.

Rather than trying to get to where you are going the long way around by walking along the surface of your piece of paper (the four-dimensional space/time manifold), you access the dimension of emotion and move through that dimension to access the reality that you want to be living in.

You can either try to get to where you are going by hustling in the dimensions of space and time, or you can travel through the dimension of emotion instead to get there via a more direct route. It's like the reality that you want to experience is on the other side of the world, and instead of taking a boat trip that will take you a year along the surface of the Earth, you're going to drill through the center of the Earth so that you can get there in a day.

Let me try to put this as simply as possible.

Your current life exists at a certain set of multidimensional coordinates. You exist in a certain place in space, at a certain point in time, you are experiencing a certain frequency of emotion, a certain temperature, a certain electrical charge, a certain magnetic field, etc. These are all the 'points of data' that make up your reality right now. If we were to chart you on a 12 dimensional graph with those sets of data, we would have 12 sets of coordinates that show us exactly what your life is right now. Those points of data tell us everything about your life.

Well, LoA and manifesting tell you that the reality that you want to experience already exists at another set of coordinates. There exists a reality in which the things you want are already happening and you simply need to get to those coordinates (reality transurfing), or you need to magnetically attract the things that you want - which already exist at another coordinate - into your reality (law of attraction), or your thoughts and emotions can spawn the existence of something that matches the energy that you are putting out (manifesting).

All that you need to do is to get yourself to the coordinates of the thing that you want to experience, so that you and the thing that you want to experience can exist in the same space, time, emotion, etc. You need to get to that 'place'.

LoA, manifesting, and reality transferring are then based on one concept; that you have more access to - and more control over - your movement through the dimension of emotion than you have over your movement through any other dimension. You may not be able to consciously get yourself to the spatial coordinates of your other, better life (because they exist in a 'space' beyond this physical world - an alternate physical reality), and you can't control your movement through the complex dimension of time, but what you CAN do is get yourself to the same emotional coordinates of the life that you want to experience and - by doing so - help move yourself into that reality or bring that reality into your experience.

Your goal is to align your coordinates with the coordinates of what you want, and the dimension that you have the most control over is that of emotions. So, let's put yourself into the emotional state that you would be in if you had the things that you want, because by staying in that emotional space you can be most aligned with the things that you want and you can come to experience them that much sooner. Basically - get yourself into alignment with ANY of the coordinates of the reality you want to live in, and the others will start falling into place, and since the dimension that you can most actively control is that of emotion, we should start with that.

If you try to get there through hustle and grind in the 3D world alone without adjusting your emotions to the world you want to live in, then it will take you exponentially longer to get there because no part of you is yet in alignment with that reality, but by relaxing into the emotions held by the version of you that is already there you can basically bring it all into your reality infinitely easier.

You want your coordinates to match the coordinates of what you want to experience. Right now, you exist at [1, 1, 1, 1, 1] where the first three numbers are your spatial coordinates, the fourth number is your temporal coordinate, and the 5th number is your emotional coordinate. Your goal is to get to [9, 9, 9, 9, 9]. It is extremely difficult to force your movements through the first four dimensions, but if you can get yourself right now to the coordinates [1, 1, 1, 1, 9], then everything else will start happening and falling into place naturally.

Get yourself to the emotional coordinates of what you want, because that is the dimension you have the most control over, and then you will be magnetically attracting the reality that you want into your experience because the version of you that exists at that emotional coordinate as its set point is also connected to all the other ideal coordinates of the other dimensions that you are trying to experience.

This is - in my perspective - the multi-dimensional explanation of how LoA works. You are creating a wormhole through the dimension of emotion to get you to a far-off set of space-time coordinates very quickly.

B - The Psychological Side

Fortunately, as I mentioned, you don't need to buy into any of that to make sense of all this or to get started with Manifesting or LoA, because the practices and techniques that you will use just make sense at the psychological level - regardless of where they originate from or what weird principles of a quantum reality they might rely on.

When I started my inner healing journey I had only three words - 'unconditional self-love' - to guide me. I discovered the concept of unconditional self-love and became determined to learn and master it. Those words and that guidance came to me from a spiritual source that I wasn't yet ready to open up to or believe in specifically. I followed the advice and guidance because I knew that it was sound and solid advice regardless of the fact that it came from a source with beliefs I didn't resonate with.

In other words, I knew that learning unconditional self-love could only help me and make my life better, regardless of the fact that this guidance came to me from a spiritual source that I didn't feel fully comfortable with. It didn't matter to me that it was a 'spiritual' concept because it made sense to me at the practical, psychological level, so I moved forward with it, allowing myself to do something that felt a little uncomfortable to my rational mind. The more that I followed the guidance and lessons, the better things got and the more that I started understanding and resonating with the spiritual elements of it. I only eventually started opening up to the spiritual elements because of the undeniable effect that this concept had on me at the practical level.

That is how you can approach LoA and Manifesting as well. It doesn't matter if it's spiritually true because by following the guidance and exercises of these practices, your life will get better at the practical level anyway.

We've spoken a fair bit about the subconscious cycles that are happening inside of us all the time and the co-creation cycles that are always happening between ourselves and the outer world. Our emotions are more in control of our actions than we realize, and our lives, circumstances, and relationships are determined by those actions, which then affect our emotions, affecting our decisions, affecting our circumstances, and around and around we go. A looping cycle where our inner world affects our decisions on the outer world, and where our outer world affects the state of our inner world, thereby guiding our decisions. This is the concept of co-creation. One hand draws the other in an eternal cosmic dance.

So, is it truly any wonder or mystical miracle to recognize that adjusting our emotions will help adjust our attitude, which will then help us make better decisions and form better connections so that we can - more smoothly and confidently - move in the direction that we want to go in? Is there anything weird about the idea that a person who is happy, optimistic, hopeful, and passionate will have more chances at achieving their goals than someone who is bitter, resentful, angry, and rude?

It's obvious that the person who is in control of their emotions and living in that higher emotional state of love as opposed to the lower state of fear will be more willing and able to notice the opportunities that come their way, to work towards them gleefully, to take advantage of them, etc., and that the bitter person might be presented with the very same opportunities in their life, but would end up pushing them away or not taking advantage of them because their energy, attitude, and emotions were not conducive to motivated action and were unpleasant for others to be around. It's going to take effort to accomplish things in your life, and those with a better attitude and emotional state will be more ready and able to put in the effort to get there. It starts with your emotions.

As far as 'Reality Transurfing' goes, let me point out that these two imaginary people (the optimistic lover and the pessimistic misanthrope) - even if they are coworkers two desks away - are actually living in completely different realities in a very real way. The optimistic and happy person lives in a world where people are generally good and kind, where things generally work out ok, where hard work is nothing to be afraid of, etc... This is his mentality in his head. This is how he looks at the world and how he experiences his day-to-day life. The bitter and resentful person experiences things differently. He believes that people are naturally rotten, that the world is always out to get him, that things never work out, etc. That is his reality.

They both live in the same world physically and temporally. They are right next to each other, but they both experience a drastically different version of the world as a result of their emotional energy and disposition. This experience of the world reinforces itself by affecting the decisions that each of these people will make in their lives. The hopeful one will be trusting and excited to try new opportunities and the bitter one will refuse to take chances.

You probably already notice this in your own life, if you are attempting to be positive while your friends and family constantly find reasons to be upset. One of my best friends lives in that negative reality where everyone is terrible, whereas I live in a reality where everyone who acts poorly is actually in pain. His reality is one where people are malicious and apathetic, mine is one where everyone is just love covered up by pain. We live in two different universes, even when we are sitting across a table from one another.

A shift in a bitter man's mentality could completely turn his whole life around, but he is too stuck in his negative model of the universe to try, and he is stuck in that mental model because he is still in emotional pain that he doesn't know how to confront and release. It all stems from unresolved emotions.

By shifting your emotional state and practicing staying in higher emotional frequencies, you can jumpstart the upwards spiral that will completely change your life and deliver you into a new world where you can see how people really are generally good, kind and loving, rather than your current world where everyone is just awful.

Every moment of every day, you are moving either up or down on this emotional/spiritual spiral staircase. The higher that you rise by focusing on your own emotions and inner well-being, the more ready, able, and willing you will be to hop on all the opportunities that life gives you, but when you allow yourself to slip downwards you will fall into victim mentality and you will become more and more passive in terms of directing your life - allowing this negative cycle to continue, grow, and amplify.

The reason I use the spiral staircase metaphor is because it takes time to move from one level to the next. It's not a day-to-day thing. Moving up a single step on the staircase doesn't change your reality, but getting to the next level of the spiral will. It's a practice that works on a long-term scale. Making yourself super happy one day and then wondering "well, why didn't anything amazing happen?" is not how this works. We don't expect that you raise your emotions one day and everything changes. You need to make sure that you are - as much as possible and over the long run - working your way up this spiral instead of down, and change will slowly start happening in your life. Your life will always reflect - with some delayed effect - where you are at on this spiral staircase and the direction you are moving in.

Additionally, on the psychological side of this is the simple idea that programming yourself to expect something will make you more likely to take action towards it. You can't achieve something you don't believe is possible (not intentionally, anyway), because you won't work towards it. But if you convince yourself that - say - you becoming wealthy is inevitable, then you will always be optimistically looking for how it is going to play out and you will move towards it more and more every day, jumping on every possible opportunity to make it happen. If, on the other hand, you believe that you will always be poor and that nothing can change that, then you will stay in that lane. You will never jump on an opportunity to become rich because you won't believe that it can work. You'll stay comfortably numb in the life that you are already living.

By consciously manipulating your emotions and beliefs you can help ensure that you consistently move in the direction of the reality that you want, instead of allowing yourself to slip into a passive victim role in your own life.

If you believe life will always be terrible and that everyone is malicious, then you will take angry, bitter, defensive action that will lead you nowhere. If you raise your emotions, however, and adopt the attitude that your life is destined to be awesome and that everyone is good and kind at their cores, you will take action based on that mentality that will help you achieve what you want to achieve.

No spirituality necessary. It's all psychology.

***

I want to add in a little note about what it means to be 'multi-dimensional' and how two things can be true at the same time - how we are all just looking at the same phenomena through different lenses.

If you start acting according to the principles of LoA and you begin to start seeing results, how will you determine whether it worked at the spiritual level or only at the psychological level? Which is the true story? Did it work only because of the psychology or was it actually energy? Which was primary? Where did the real magic happen?

Well... it doesn't matter, and there's no difference, and... the answer is 'both'. It is simultaneously true that it worked because your psychological and emotional improvement created practical opportunities and progress and it's ALSO true that, energetically, you became more aligned with the reality you wanted to experience and naturally started gravitating to it.

Both are accurate and true explanations of what just happened, and it's just about what lens you are using when you look at it. Acknowledging this is how the skeptics among us start opening up to these spiritual concepts. It doesn't contradict the physical and practical explanation, it's a higher dimensional understanding that overlaps with it.

C - The Grand Paradox

The main thing that people fail to understand about Manifesting and LoA is that it is based entirely on a paradox where the only way to make it work in your favor is by not trying to make it work in your favor. When you understand this paradox, it becomes obvious why you should absolutely be living your life according to these principles, regardless of whether or not the spiritual elements of these phenomena are real.

Here's how to manifest things - according to the spiritual approach.

In order to bring what you want into your reality; you first need to train yourself to feel the way that you would feel if you had the thing that you are trying to create. You have to put yourself into the same emotional coordinates that you would be in if you were already experiencing that which you were trying to manifest.

Once you can fully visualize and feel the end result, the next step is to let go of the expectation of that outcome. The more that you desperately cling on to the need for this thing to be reality, the more that you energetically push it away. The idea is that the energy of desiring something is the exact opposite energy of having it. Therefore, the more that you focus on your desire for this thing, the more that you are putting out an energy that actually repels this thing from coming into your life.

So, on the one hand, you need to already feel like you have it and, on the other hand, you need to not care at all - to not truly be attached to - whether or not you have it or will ever get it.

The secret paradox, then, is this: By the time that you are ready to attract and have the thing that you want, it won't matter to you if you have it or not, and it is ONLY from that emotional place that you can manifest what you want into reality.

By the time you are in manifesting mode, you will already feel as good as if you had it and you won't be concerned about getting it... so what difference does it make? You'll already be happy.

The secret you just discovered then is that the only way to get what you want is to just be happy, unafraid, and unconditionally loving while you don't have it. The better you feel about life, the better your life will be and THEN you can get what you thought you wanted. This is in complete contrast to the way that most of us have lived our lives so far - where we are constantly trying to attain things in the outside world that we think will make us happy. We have just reversed the whole way that we look at life and realized that working on ourselves internally is the only way to truly get everything that we want.

Beautiful. Simple. Elegant.

Basically, you can't con the universe. In order to manifest your dreams, you must first achieve unconditional self-love and true surrender, but you can't try to cheat and pretend to achieve unconditional self-love and surrender for the sake of getting what you want. It has to be real and legitimate, and when you achieve unconditional self-love and surrender, nothing else will matter. You will be at peace with life and the universe and you'll just be happy watching to see how things play out. You may even realize that the thing you thought you wanted isn't something that you want anymore. You will begin realizing that 'Law of Attraction' may actually just be a clever joke of the universe to trick you into becoming the best version of yourself, and you'll be alright with that.

If you want to experience the best life possible, you need to get to the emotional state of bliss regardless of where you are at in your life, and once you are in a state of bliss you won't be so determined to get the thing that you wanted in the first place (because you're already happy and truly content), and THEN you will be able to manifest that thing that you thought you wanted in the first place – or better.

The big and secret lesson behind all of this is that you don't actually want the thing that you think you want. What you ACTUALLY want is merely the emotional experience that you think this external thing will give you. So, let's focus on getting you that emotional experience FIRST - before you have the thing you are trying to manifest. Nothing else matters, and when you are living in that emotional experience already, you will be ready to receive the thing you thought was going to give you that experience in the first place, but you may or may not still want the same thing anyway. By that point, you'll be a different person altogether.

D - Scripting

There are many methods for Manifesting that you can learn. Some of the common favorites are visualizations and journaling, and some more esoteric things like the 'two cup method' where you pour water from one cup into another to represent the shift from one reality to another, etc.

I'm going to share with you the method that I have found to be most effective at the psychological and - so far - at the practical levels. Yes... my manifestations do seem to be coming true.

My first round of scripted manifestations - that I created several years ago - did not come to be as true as the ones that I made more recently, because I was not yet at the right emotional space to manifest from, nor did I understand enough about the process to make it work. I was still in a desperate mentality of desire at the time, and I still looked at manifesting as this magical silver bullet that could bring your wildest desires to life in inexplicable ways. So, the manifesting script that I made a few years ago has only partially come to fruition (but I'm still on my way to making it my reality) whereas the script that I wrote out four months ago is coming true VERY quickly, because I understand more how this all works.

As I've been saying for all your spiritual practices... you have to understand them at a practical level first in order to make them work. If you ONLY do them from the spiritual side - expecting that the universe is going to drop everything you want into your lap because you asked or prayed for it - you will find yourself constantly disappointed. If, on the other hand, you come to understand the universal laws and principles behind these practices, you can make use of them in a way that will benefit your life, regardless of whether the spiritual elements of it are real or not, and only from there can you allow the spiritual versions of these principles to impact your life.

The method we will use is known as 'scripting' and is pretty simply exactly what it sounds like. You are going to write up a script about what it is that you want to happen in your life. You will literally script it into reality.

There are many ways to script for manifesting. For this method, the form of the script will be a thank you letter written from the future. You are going to compose a letter of gratitude to someone/something that has helped you already achieve the things that you are trying to manifest into reality.

Step #1 is to pick who you will write this letter to. Maybe there is a role model who helped inspire you to get to where you want to go, and your dream/visualization for the context of this letter is about meeting this person in the future and thanking them. Maybe it's a parent who helped you achieve your goals. Maybe it's someone who passed away that you will get to thank in a dream one day. Maybe it's a celebrity who encouraged you and inspired you. When I first heard about this method, the person had written a letter to Abraham Hicks, thanking her for teaching her about manifesting and all that, and the person had written this letter also in the hopes of manifesting an opportunity to meet Mrs. Hicks and thank her for it. This person did in fact get to read that letter to Abraham Hicks one day, by the way.

(For those of you unaware, yes... Abraham Hicks is a woman. Long story... Her real name is Esther.)

If you have no-one in particular to write to and thank, you can always go with 'the universe', God, your higher self, your 'spirit guides' or whatever resonates with you on that end. That's what I did for my last round of scripting. I wrote to my higher self and spirit guides.

Step #2 is to begin your letter by thanking this person in general for the role they played in helping you achieve what you are about to tell them about and to thank them for the opportunity to meet with them and to tell them all of this. Enter into this letter with the emotion of gratitude and the visualization that you actually get to read this letter to them.

Step #3 is to plan out the various elements of your life and have some vision in mind. You can deal with any or all areas like relationships, career, health, spiritual fulfillment, etc. you are going to describe in as much detail as possible the full layout of the life you want to live.

Here's the key though... it is NOT about the things you are writing about directly. If you're writing about a big house, a nice car, the perfect spouse, etc., that's all well and good, but none of that actually matters. What matters in manifesting, remember, is the emotions. You are trying to attune yourself emotionally to how you will feel when you have the things that you are writing about. So, the goal of the letter is to focus on the feelings as much as possible.

Saying "Thank you so much for helping me get this car! It's so shiny and pretty. It has really nice rims, etc." is ok. But saying "Oh my god... I feel so free and confident when I'm driving this car... it's amazing! I never imagined that I could feel so at one with the road and to experience the thrill of this kind of speed and the roaring of that engine" is 1,000x times better.

Do you see the difference between the two statements? The first one focuses on the physical and material object whereas the other focuses on how being in that scenario will make you feel. They are two entirely different statements, even though they are focused on the same content.

The details of your manifestations are likely never going to be exactly how things play out, but when your focus is on the emotion first, then you can be more open as to how these emotions actually come to happen in your life. You will be more willing and alert to follow the direction that the universe shows you, as opposed to trying to force things to happen in a certain way. You are manifesting emotions, not specific physical things or experiences.

As much as possible then, for each area of your life you want to express immense gratitude, in as much detail as possible, for how having your dream life feels. Let the feelings fuel the visualizations and make sure that the visualizations and the goals are as lofty as you can imagine. Don't hold anything back! This is a practice of connecting to the greatest and most amazing feelings you can possibly attach yourself to. This is basically an exercise for practicing happiness, joy, love, bliss, excitement, etc. If you try to turn this process into anything more or less than that, you will miss the point entirely and will never experience the benefits.

So, you SHOULD aim for the biggest goals that you can imagine, BUT... there is a caveat to that. Remember, you cannot achieve what you don't believe is possible. If you are scripting about things that you believe are impossible then you won't be able to bring those things into reality. More importantly, you won't be able to truly connect to the emotions of having them during your scripting because they will seem so ridiculous. Your logical mind will get in the way. So, you need to aim big, on the one hand, but you also need to either stay within the realm of what you already believe is possible, or else you need to work on your limiting beliefs to expand the limits of what you think is possible. Really, you'll need to do both. Breaking limiting beliefs is a huge part of the healing journey and the manifesting process.

Write out everything that you want to manifest in every area of your life, with as much detail as possible (be very descriptive), but where the focus is on how these things will make you feel, and make sure that you stay within the realm of what you believe can actually happen - while at the same time staying unattached to how it happens. Try not to include in your script anything too specific about how this comes to pass or how it has to play out. Leave it open ended as much as possible so that you don't accidentally restrict yourself to one very specific scenario, which won't help you take action in the future when you are presented with opportunities that don't match that exact thing.

Once your letter is written, your goal is to read the letter out loud once or twice every day for 21-30 days. You want to program these words and the emotions attached to them into your subconscious brain. You are going to spend 21-30 days training your brain to think and feel as if this has already happened. You are going to practice feeling as if you are already in that reality. Try to enjoy the act of reading it as much as possible by actually putting yourself into the feelings you are moving towards. Read it as if these things have really already happened and you are truly thanking this person for helping you get there. Really play it out. Get into it. Go for the Oscar!

Remember... you can't con the universe and you want to be using this exercise in a practical way that will have an effect on your life regardless of whether or not the spiritual concept of manifesting is real.

You should be performing this exercise FIRSTLY and MOSTLY just because it feels good. That's it. You are practicing feeling good and being positive because just doing so will improve your life. Being more positive and feeling good will help you take better action in your life and that's all you need to know for now. If and when you see how amazingly this works, THEN you can start considering the spiritual elements more fully, but for now let's stay grounded in reality.

Make sure that you are performing this from the right energy and intention. If you're doing this because you desperately need what you wrote down to happen in order to be happy, then you are actually practicing desire, attachment and desperation, and that will push you further and further away from the things that you are trying to manifest. It's all about energy. Practice positive energy in yourself because you prefer to be happy and optimistic than bitter and resentful and because you acknowledge that an improved attitude and demeanor (along with the reprogramming of your subconscious mind to expect success) will lead to progress in your life.

After 21-30 days, put it away. You're done. Go on with your life, simply feeling better because you spent this time practicing happiness, and then believe, keep some faith, and most importantly, keep your eyes open for opportunities to move forward towards the things you scripted.

For example, a few months ago when I did this process for myself, part of what I scripted was about the expansion of my coaching business and the development of a few sources of passive income with it. At the time, I had no intentions of writing a book - let alone two - nor did I have any ideas of what I would write or any business plans around them. Here I am, a few months later, putting the finishing touches on my second book that truly just flowed out of me without much 'effort' on my part, because I stayed open to the intuitions that would come to me at any time.

I didn't know HOW I was going to achieve business expansion and passive income; I just knew that I would. That way, I didn't end up having to try to force the universe to comply with my will in overly specific ways. Instead, I was able to just receive whatever guidance and intuition would be shown to me, which turned out to be these books (...and other things). I programmed myself for the energy of freedom and success, gave the general guidelines, and waited for my intuition to tell me how to get there. When my intuition gave me direction, I was ready, willing, and able to follow it and - even when I started what my intuition told me to do - I still had no idea how it was all going to play out. Things started falling into place one at a time, but if I had waited for the whole picture to reveal itself, I never would have taken any action at all. I just stayed in the moment and did what felt right at the time.

The universe was giving me pieces to the answer one at a time... and not in any regular order. I didn't know how the pieces were going to fit together. There were courses and materials I bought six months ago that seemed like a waste of money until they all of a sudden fell into place of what I need now. I had to just trust my gut and go with things that felt right at the time.

Also, the universe didn't just drop this stuff in my lap. I had to work... a lot. Putting together these two books, learning about how to publish them, how to put together eBooks and audiobooks and deliver them through an automated system to people all over the world, learning how to make ads designed to promote books, building the new websites and funnels, attaining ISBNs and barcodes, etc. All of this took a lot of work and it was 'hard'. But it was also super easy in the sense that I didn't really have to plan any of it out. I just kept on moving forward with whatever was shown to me in the moment – one step at a time without needing to know the end results - and things just kept working out on their own.

Two days after I started writing my first book, I saw the perfect ad for a perfect course about how to turn a book into the center of your coaching business and build your whole business around it. I was naturally shown the guidance I needed to develop a new business model around the thing that my intuition had told me to do. That helped me get this far in terms of building the next stage of my business. Then, just yesterday I was pushed to another course about how to self-publish for best results and run FB ads for a book and all that.

These things were basically presented to me magically. Like I said... eventually the spiritual elements of this start seeming undeniable, when you notice the miraculous ways that these things play themselves out on the physical plane. I used a 'magical', higher dimensional law to get me on the path, but you will always be able to find a practical and reasonable explanation of how it all happens also. Whether this was magic or hard work or both is simply a matter of perspective. I know that the law of attraction played a role, and I also know that I worked my ass off - not just over these last few months but throughout my life - to get myself to this point.

Bit by bit, I allowed things to fall into place on their own. I knew where I wanted to end up emotionally, and I allowed the universe to show me how to get there. Then, of course, I needed to step up to the challenge and put in the work... but it's about finding that balance between what you can control and what you can't.

I'm now on my way to fulfilling at least that 'career' section of my latest script, in a way that I could not have possibly envisioned when I wrote my script in the first place.

So... keep the details open, but make the emotions solid. Then, keep your eyes open and wait for the opportunities, guidance, and intuition to present themselves. If you are free from fear and open to the direction the universe points you in, you will take the right action when the time presents itself, and you will move towards your goals infinitely faster than if you tried to beat the world into submission through sheer force of will.

That's all!

Happy scripting!

REMINDER

Quick interruption. Are you enjoying this book? Are you finding it helpful? Do you believe that it can help others and that the ideas in this book are worth sharing?

Do you believe that the world would be a better place if more people understood the things you are learning here and if more people dove into this healing?

If so, **please** take a minute right now and go leave a review for this book on Amazon or on GoodReads. This will go a long way to helping others know that there is valuable information here.

Then, please consider making a post about this book on social media.

Thank you so much for taking the time! It truly means a lot to me and it will help spread these important lessons and push us collectively to a brighter world. You sharing this book with someone might be the very thing that turns their whole life around.

A digital copy of this book can be purchased at http://BenjyShererCoaching.com/mhbook. Physical copies and Kindle versions can be found on Amazon and some other online retailers. Audiobooks are also available.

Now, back to the book.

11

How This All Fits Into The Healing Journey

Well... that's 10!

I mean... with all the extra sections and explanations I hope that you already got so much more out of this book than you ever expected to.

> I promise that if you spend the next 30 days applying each of the Mind Hacks we went through in this book, it will accelerate your healing process 1,000 fold. I dare you!

Simply by absorbing and embodying the wisdom behind why these mind hacks could work will give you a huge foundation of knowledge that will help you on your journey.

These Mind Hacks, however, are meant to be used as part of a whole reprogramming of your mind that you need to do when trying to heal your emotional wounds. They are all 'part of a balanced breakfast', if you will. These Mind Hacks are tools that you are using to help push your brain in a particular direction as you work to undo years of fear-based programming that you have built up as defense mechanisms to help you not feel the unresolved emotions that you carry within you. You can't just reprogram the brain, however, unless you also work on removing the old programming. This book focused on building the new programming, but first (and/or simultaneously) you're going to have to work on undoing the old programming and building a new set of emotional muscles.

The healing journey that my clients go on with me (which you can learn more about in my other book *Feelings First Shadow Work* or my 8-week Emotional Mastery Course by the same name) has three overall stages.

The first stage is where you learn about the real healing and begin to undo the old programming of the past. You start by building a strong emotional foundation to make sure that you are ready to dive into the healing and stay emotionally stable while you confront your emotions. It seems obvious... but most people never do this. Even therapists do not generally prepare their clients for the journey by giving them tools to develop emotional strength before they start.

So, you begin by learning more about your emotions - how they work, how they connect to energy, how they connect to your thoughts and your sensations and all about the subconscious cycles that have been going on - so that you can finally notice and observe them and thereby start interrupting the old cycles and thought patterns that were keeping you going in circles. You also work on building some tools, habits, and techniques that will keep you feeling as good as possible as often as possible and teach you how to pick yourself up out of the darkness as quickly as possible whenever you fall into it.

Basically, you stabilize your emotions and raise your emotional average (how you feel on a day-to-day basis) as well as your emotional awareness and mindfulness, making sure that you have a solid footing on which to stand while you begin your journey.

Next, you learn how to heal emotions subconsciously, meaning that - for the most part - you don't need to know exactly what you are healing in the moment in order to heal it. Your goal is to connect with the unresolved emotions directly by connecting more to what you are feeling in the moment. Those unresolved emotions that are presenting themselves to you in a given moment are actually connected to a whole range of different memories and traumas. It's not about healing specific memories and traumas directly, it's about dealing with the unresolved emotions and releasing the memories as a byproduct. It is more intangible than a direct connection to one specific memory. It is simply a 'pool' of unresolved emotions of a particular frequency, and you need to learn how to tap into that pool and start draining it. When you confront a single emotion, you help to heal 100 memories.

So, you learn how to tap into that pool, thereby breaking the barrier between your head and your heart that you have built up over the years, and developing the tools and skills that you are going to use from here on out to confront your unresolved emotions when they come up on their own. You learn how to turn any moment of emotional distress into a moment of healing - instead of a moment of stuffing more feelings down on top of the unresolved pile.

Now that you have a sense of stability and the basic tools you will need to use when you get triggered into past pain, you can begin step #3 where you do the real conscious healing work. In this step, you are going to learn how to work from the top down to build emotional strength naturally and slowly allow your unresolved emotions to start releasing themselves on their own.

'From the top down' means that you are not going to spend your time seeking out trauma and trying to deal with your core wounds first, directly, or even really at all. Instead, you are going to learn how to simply confront whatever comes up in the moment. You are not going to start by dealing with the heaviest core trauma inside of you, because you are not yet strong enough to deal with that core trauma anyway.

Until you learn - for example - how not to get angry when someone cuts you off in traffic, then you are certainly not ready to deal with the nasty stuff that happened to you when you were five years old that programmed that anger response into you in the first place. Instead, you are going to start with the things that trigger you in your day-to-day life, and you are going to learn how to handle them better in a way that will help you release past trauma instead of continuing to stuff it aside. As you do this, you will get stronger and better at confronting the emotions that come up, while we slowly strip away layer after layer of defense mechanisms, allowing you to get down to the core issues gradually. This is a much safer and more efficient way of clearing out your past pain.

So, you are going to work from the top down. Let's deal with the smaller things first and develop the tools, skills, and muscles you will need to conquer the deeper traumas when you get there. This allows the healing to happen in a smooth and natural way. Your goal isn't to hunt down and focus on all the horrible things that happened to you. Instead, your goal is merely to learn how to feel as good as possible as often as possible and to learn how to finally listen to your heart when it sends you unresolved emotions to be healed.

Your heart is telling you about your past pain every time you get triggered and the most efficient way to heal and release it is NOT by analyzing it through the mind, but rather by learning how to speak the emotional language of the heart, bypassing the brain (more or less) entirely and starting from the surface layers of pain that you are experiencing in that very moment, so that you can start peeling away the layers and get back down to your core incrementally, smoothly, and naturally. That is the 'top down' healing method of my *Feelings First* approach.

Therapists work from the bottom up - trying to find and analyze your core trauma to help you understand why you're getting triggered in your day-to-day life. *Feelings First Shadow Work* does it in the completely opposite way, learning how to use your daily triggers to point you in the direction of your healing, while you slowly follow the breadcrumb trail down until the core wounds reveal and/or release themselves on their own.

It is a much simpler, more intuitively progressive (it builds on itself naturally), and more painless process. You focus on enjoying life more and getting better and stronger at confronting uncomfortable emotions, instead of focusing on all the reasons you think you're traumatized and trying to analyze them. This way, you're never dealing with more than you can handle and you are just enjoying life more and more every day as you master your emotions and move in the right direction.

That is stage one of my 8-week course. You build a foundation, break the barriers, and learn the skills that you need so that you can start a natural process of undoing trauma progressively.

The Mind Hacks you learned in this book, however, relate more to stage two of your inner healing journey, which is all about programming the new positive paradigms into yourself. While stage one is all about starting to undo the old programming, stage two is all about building the new programming, because no matter how much 'stage one healing' you do, if you don't give your brain an alternate route to go down, then you will eventually slip back into your old programming. That's just the way it goes.

Water always flows to the lowest point. It gravitates to the most natural path of least resistance, and the same is true of your brain and your behavior when you get emotionally triggered. You have spent a lifetime paving certain pathways in your brain as responses to certain emotions and whenever you get triggered, distracted, and sent into 'auto-pilot' mode because your emotions pull you out of mindfulness for a moment, you will naturally head down the pathways that have been paved the most.

Tip-toe over your old programming as much as you want... Until you begin actively paving new pathways you will never be free of your old cycles and defense mechanisms.

This is stage two, then. Paving the new pathways in your brain that you can switch into as you start shifting out of your old fear-based paradigm. This is the stuff that these mind hacks are best used for. They can help remind you to do some of the healing and they can keep you in the best mind-state for them, staying positive and optimistic while you go through your healing and growth.

So, these steps need to happen together and in order for them to have the largest effect possible. Sure... If you do everything piecemeal and individually, it will still have benefits for you. There's no doubt about that. But it won't have the full transformative impact that it could if you go through the whole process properly. If you do all the stage one healing but never reprogram new pathways for yourself, you'll keep slipping back into your old habits, but if you only build new pathways and never learn to heal the unresolved emotions, you'll never truly settle into your new paradigm. Additionally, if you don't do these things in the proper order, it will be very hard for your mind to put all the pieces together. The healing process we go through in my course is very carefully curated to make sure that everything happens as naturally as possible.

Stage two involves a lot of elements of reprogramming your brain, including (but not limited to):

- Learning how to connect to your heart space and truly start living from a place of emotion, passion, and love.

- Letting go of the fear of expressing yourself and being yourself.

- Learning how to put up healthy boundaries against behavior that doesn't serve you, WHILE learning to be unconditionally loving and compassionate (self-love comes first, but you love others unconditionally as well for your own benefit).

- How to give love to others in a safe and healthy way that is not based on self-betrayal.

- How to adjust your physical environment to support the inner healing journey that you have been going on.

- How to stay in the now moment - allowing you to let go of the past (which is where all guilt and shame is held) and the false imagined negative versions of the future (where worry and stress stem from).

- How to trust your intuition so that you can stop over-analyzing everything and relax into your life (people love to talk about this but no-one shows you how to do it! Trusting your intuition is a muscle that needs to be exercised and trained).

- How to bridge the gap between spirituality and science in your mind so that you can start living without inner conflict around this new approach to your life.

- And more...

These are all things that you work on in stage two of the healing, because having these new perspectives, programs, and beliefs in place is how you will avoid slipping back into old patterns and finally settle into this new version of yourself and of the world that you are getting used to. This is where these Mind Hacks will be most useful.

The very last stage of this healing is what most people mistakenly start with... dealing with the core trauma that is left over. Most people approach this inner healing as an intellectual activity where their first goal is to track down the worst things that happened to them and try to rationally make sense of them so that they can finally move on. Unfortunately, simply remembering where your trauma came from - and even understanding how it's still affecting you - is not going to allow you to truly release the emotions around it because...

HEALING IS NOT AN INTELLECTUAL ACTIVITY. It is an emotional one.

You can't solve a problem of the heart from the head. It's just not going to happen.

Besides, those core wounds are the heaviest weights of emotional distress that you are carrying around with you, and it wouldn't make sense to try and tackle them at the beginning. You're not strong enough yet. So, hopefully you can now understand why things need to happen in a particular order for this healing to be as effective as possible.

You begin by building the foundation of emotional strength and the skills you will need, so that you can start working from the top down, developing the emotional muscles and getting stronger and stronger at confronting uncomfortable emotions whenever they arise naturally. While continuing to build those muscles and undo the layers of fear-based programming you start replacing the old programming with new programming founded on unconditional self-love and inner-growth. ONLY once you have built enough muscle, cleared away enough programming, and developed the new paradigm that you will shift into, do you turn your attention to whatever is left over and still anchoring you into your deepest wounds, because only by the end of this process are you ready to truly undo those ties and lift those anchors.

Hopefully, you can see how this is a much more natural and efficient process than the traditional therapy route, and yet a much more direct, effective, and practical approach than the 'spiritual energy healing' route. It Is about emotional training. You are trying to strengthen your emotional muscles, tools, and skills. Or... I sometimes liken it to learning to surf. You need to learn how to ride the biggest emotional waves without falling off your board, so that you can handle anything life throws at you with grace and ease and keep moving forward towards the life you want to live.

If you have been on an inner healing or spiritual journey for any significant amount of time and haven't seen the grand transformation you are looking for, it is likely because you haven't been incorporating all of these steps, or not doing them in the proper order. I've had clients who had been in therapy for 30 years make more progress with me in 8 weeks than they ever did before because they had long ago exhausted the limits of what a conceptual understanding of their trauma could offer and they never moved on to the actual emotional healing. I've also had clients who had tried every spiritual healing technique in the book over a span of decades, but were still suffering, and finally overcame their pain with the *Feelings First* methods, because spiritual healing methods – despite making them feel good for brief periods - never gave them the emotional tools that they needed for those spiritual lessons to truly get grounded into them.

I'm not saying that therapy and spiritual healing methods are useless. What I am saying is that they are relatively useless IF you don't combine them with tools and techniques to master your emotions directly. There are various layers of your experience of reality. Your conscious experience is a fairly low grade 'reality', your spiritual reality is high up there (beyond your physical experiences), and right in between the two is your emotional reality. If you want to shift into the spiritual, high minded, free, purpose-filled kind of life you are longing to live in and embody, then you will need to master your emotions directly so that you can keep progressing and reach that next level.

Most people, however, stay stuck in the bottom realm or try to skip right to the top one - leading them inevitably to a drastic roller coaster where half their lives are spent trying to pretend like they are all about 'love and light', while they are simultaneously still getting triggered every day into fear, anger, resentment, jealousy, anxiety, stress or desire. If you are still getting triggered into those emotions on a regular basis by your day-to-day life, then you need to learn the emotional tools to turn those moments into healing experiences, instead of just trying to soothe them away or avoid them.

Without developing direct emotional mastery and strength, you will never escape the cycles that you are living in, and teaching you how to do that as easily, efficiently, quickly, and painlessly as possible is what the *Feelings First* course and approach is designed for!

12

Next Steps

If that three stage process that I just laid out makes sense to you - if you want to learn and master everything I just listed out as quickly and painlessly as possible - there are two best ways to proceed from here.

Hopefully you have already read my other book, *Feelings First Shadow Work*. If you have, then you are already aware of this process and you already have a good sense of how these Mind Hacks fit into it. If not, I highly suggest that you start there. It will give you an immense amount of foundational knowledge about your emotions and this healing journey and how to piece it all together.

> You can find out more about the book over here:
> http://BenjyShererCoaching.com/ffbook

If you've already read that, however, and/or if you just want to dive into this healing journey and come out the other side as quickly, efficiently and painlessly as possible, then you should look into my 8-week course where I will take you step-by-step through every last bit of conceptual information, every last skill, practice, exercise, and lesson that you will need to completely master your emotions, in a carefully curated order to make it as easy and understandable as possible.

Things like anxiety, fear, guilt, PTSD, suicidal thoughts and tendencies, being a work-a-holic, codependency, overwhelm... These are all things that I have seen my clients overcome by putting into practice the methods that I teach, and if you have made it this far in the book then I can more or less guarantee that this course is right for you, will resonate with you, and will lead you into a better life. There is no way that you could have bothered getting to the end of this book if my methods weren't right for you. So, if you're reading these words, you know that it will be a good fit.

I assure you, every day spent before doing this healing is a wasted day compared to what's on the other side.

Hope to see you there soon!

You can find out more about the course or sign up over here: http://BenjyShererCoaching.com/ffcourse.

13

Transformations I've Seen

Honestly... I could fill up the next 50 pages of this book with sample testimonials of what people have experienced through my course, but instead I'm going to just share with you three of my favorites. I hope that - if nothing else - these stories inspire you about what is possible for yourself - whether or not you get there with my help. I want you to know that change, inner peace, happiness, and unconditional self-love IS possible! Even for the people who have given up on it a long time ago. I PROMISE... if you devote yourself to inner healing, you can regain your love and passion for life, for yourself, and for the world again.

NO-ONE is 'too far gone'... ESPECIALLY if you are bothering to read this book and made it this far. No-one who is not already on the right path would end up reading these words.

I also promise that my course is one of the fastest ways to get there, but I mainly just want you to know that you can and will get there if you keep moving forward.

So, allow some of my clients to tell you about their experiences:

***

"A year ago, I wasn't sure if I would see today. Things got a little better through my own work. But I also knew I needed something more or I wouldn't make it. I found Benjy Sherer and took his 8 week course. After doing this course, I no longer have the continuous anxiety rolls in my chest. If I start to feel down, I have enough tools to figure out the 'why', 'what' and the 'how's to deal with it. I'm way healthier in my heart, head and soul. Benjy is compassionate, smart and is always a text, email or call away.

I'm so grateful for whatever led me to Benjy.

I looked forward to our weekly phone calls. He was so helpful with any questions or thoughts I had. I can't reiterate how much Benjy helped me and gave me the tools to help myself every day. Loved ones tell me they see such a difference in me."

— Carrie

"A few months ago, I had to face the truth: My life sucked... Though I tried my best to maintain a decent attitude and stoic demeanor, the reality was completely the opposite; I was suffering inside. For one reason or another, my life was not going the way I had envisioned when I was a kid. After what seemed like an endless downward spiral into a dark depression, I had no idea where to turn...

That's when Benjy appeared in my life. Skeptically, I decided to take a leap of faith...

I AM SO GLAD THAT I DID!!

Benjy gave me the tools to take full control over my life and destiny. He taught me how to connect with my inner self. He taught me how to trust in my intuition and find my purpose. He taught me

172

how happiness is a skill that can be developed and mastered. And he empowered me with the knowledge and tools to build lasting success as I move forward in my life.

In his awesome program, Benjy was with me every step of the way, from the theoretical concepts to the direct day-to-day application of techniques. These are habits that I will continue to use for the rest of my life - both in business and relationships.

Whether you need a massive transformation, or merely a friendly push to get your life on track, I wholeheartedly recommend working with Benjy."

— Daniel

"With recent world events I found myself spiraling and suffering from anxiety. For the first time in my life, I felt lost to my emotions not knowing where to turn. I don't remember specifically how I came upon Benjy's information but it somehow found me. I read some of his course overview information about programming and healing personal trauma and was intrigued to learn more. I knew deep down that I was seeking the tools to harness my personal power.

Benjy has managed to package so much information and exercises into this course that it is hard to look back and realize how much I have learned and how much I have grown. I don't think any amount of regular counselling sessions could have helped me heal more than this 8-week journey I most recently finished. If you are truly committed to taking responsibility for yourself and your emotions and life then this is the course for you. I can't thank Benjy enough for his sincerity and generosity of spirit that allowed me to just flow through each week and explore myself on a different level. I truly looked forward to each week and digging deeper into myself that I am now finally more at peace with myself than ever before.

By healing yourself you are giving back to the world. I truly feel like I know more about my life purpose and feel more connected and alive each and every day. Thank you, Benjy for sharing your wisdom and spirit and helping me to heal my heart and participate more fully in life and all it has to offer. Truly a life changing experience that I highly recommend. If you are reading this then you are already halfway there. You won't regret investing in yourself, I know I didn't!!!"

— Sharon

Learn more about the 8 week course at
http://BenjyShererCoaching.com/ffcourse

Or, get the *Feelings First Shadow Work* Book at
http://BenjyShererCoaching.com/ffbook.

CONCLUSION

If you are reading these words right now, then either you skipped to the end of the book because you like goodbyes... or you actually read through this whole book and followed me until the end. If that is the case, I just want to say a huge and genuine thank you on behalf of myself and the universe.

The universe thanks you because this healing journey - and attaining unconditional love for ourselves and others - is what this whole life and this whole awakening process is truly about. And I thank you because it is an amazing honor to know that my words are having an impact and that I get to be a part of your life's journey in any small way whatsoever. If this book has provided even a single nugget of information that you are going to keep with you as you move through your healing and your life, then whatever impact that has is immensely meaningful to me.

Thank you for taking the time to join me on this journey. Thank you for your patience and attention. And thank you for the work that you are doing on yourself.

Whether you choose to seek me out, join my course, read my other books, or ever have any interaction with me or my words ever again, I am honored to have joined you thus far and I wish you the very best on your healing mission.

I PROMISE you, there is more light on the other side than you ever imagined!

Stay strong. Keep up the great work.

Much love.
Yours truly,
Benjy.

WHERE ELSE CAN YOU FIND ME?

Join my FB group:
https://www.facebook.com/groups/futuremakersunited

Watch my webinar 'From Awakening to Ascended - completing the journey to 5D': www.BenjyShererCoaching.com/replay

**Get my book Feelings First Shadow Work: A Simple Approach to Self Love and Emotional Mastery: **
Http://BenjyShererCoaching.com/ffbook

Find me on YouTube as 'Benjy Sherer Coaching'.

You can still find some of my earlier writings at www.therightson.com

**Enroll in my 8-week course:
http://BenjyShererCoaching.com/ffcourse. **

Email me any time at BSherer@BenjyShererCoaching.com

I am available for lectures and speaking functions.

This book has been self-published. If any book agents or publishers are interested in this work, please get in touch.

Lightning Source UK Ltd.
Milton Keynes UK
UKHW021558040322
399574UK00007B/1625

9 781777 610227